DATE			

NATURE AND CULTURE IN D. H. LAWRENCE

Nature and Culture in
D. H. Lawrence

by

Aidan Burns

2/08

BARNES & NOBLE BOOKS
TOTOWA, NEW JERSEY

055818

First Published in the U.S.A. 1980 by
BARNES & NOBLE BOOKS
81, Adams Drive, Totowa,
New Jersey, 07512
. ISBN 0–389–20091–3

Printed in Hong Kong

Contents

Preface

This is a work of criticism which may appear unfamiliar to English readers. In it I have attempted to examine an author's work from a philosophical standpoint and to place it within a cultural tradition which includes both novelists and philosophers. In doing this I am not confusing philosophy and literary criticism. They are distinct disciplines. Nevertheless they overlap in their concerns and in many ways are mutually dependent. Lawrence himself believed this and I think he was correct.

On the Continent the philosopher as literary critic is a more familiar figure. Sartre once remarked that a novelist's technique always relates back to his metaphysics and that the critic's task is to define the latter before evaluating the former. This I think would serve as a description of what I am aiming at here.

After a short introductory chapter in which I discuss the problems of the self in philosophy and literature, I examine *Studies in Classic American Literature*, in which I think is found Lawrence's most sustained statement of his metaphysics. I have not much to say about his 'philosophical' works themselves because I do not think very highly of them. It is true that they contain some remarkable insights but as systematic expressions of a philosophy they are marred by Lawrence's inexperience in the methods of philosophical analysis. His criticism, however, is of the highest order and in *Studies* we have his most successfully sustained outline in abstract language of his views on the nature of man. This is because in his criticism of the American authors he continually refers back to certain fundamental ethical principles. In chapter 2 I have attempted to render those principles explicit.

Having established the theoretical framework, in subsequent chapters I attempt to 'apply' it to the novels. First to the two early novels, *The White Peacock* and *Sons and Lovers*. Then in chapters 4 and 5 I examine the high point of Lawrence's achievement as a novelist, *The Rainbow* and *Women in Love*. These are books to which, in Goethe's phrase, we return again and again and they are never exhausted. Their treatment here is, therefore, strictly limited to the overall purposes of this study.

There follows a short chapter on *Lady Chatterley's Lover*, which as a complete work of art I think marks a decline in Lawrence's creative powers, although it contains some of his finest writing.

Because of the philosophical perspective of this study I have continually tried to place Lawrence in relation to his philosophical contemporaries and predecessors. In this it can be seen that any cultural epoch is a whole and that, therefore, the study of the novelists and philosophers of any period illuminates both the philosophy and the literature of that period.

Throughout the work it became increasingly apparent to me that many of the problems experienced by Lawrence arose because of misunderstandings about the nature of language. I have concluded, therefore, with a short chapter on the philosophy of language, which indicates how I believe these problems might be solved.

July 1979   Aidan Burns

Acknowledgements

I would like to thank again all those friends who helped me in the preparation of this work, especially Bridget O'Toole and Walter Allen for their advice and encouragement; Brendan Murphy for reading the manuscript in its early stages and for making some valuable suggestions; Gemma Loughran who corrected it later and removed from it some of my grosser syntactical absurdities; Moya Morris for typing and other assistance in preparing the manuscript; finally, my wife Anne for assistance in all departments.

1 Introduction: Philosophy and the Novel

T. S. Eliot once expressed the view that literary criticism should always be completed by criticism from a definite moral standpoint. It is the purpose of this book to attempt such a project. Writers in England do not encourage the philosopher to intrude on their territory. They feel, and often with justice, that he gives scant attention to the text he is reading, allowing his own theories to come between him and the real spirit of the work. The philosopher/novelist like Sartre is not a figure familiar to the English reader. However, if literature is for more than *mere* enjoyment, if we can speak of books as good or bad, as life-enhancing or decadent, we are on a plane of evaluation where the work of the writer and the philosopher overlap. And put simply we should want to say that a good novel should enrich the life of the person who reads it.

The exasperation which critics and writers often feel with philosophers can partly be explained by the development of English philosophy in this century, marked as it has been by a great contraction in the scope of its interest and subject matter. It would be difficult to say just when this process began; there are few revolutions in philosophy and those things we call revolutions are often only the eruption on the surface of events which have been building up for years in the philosophical underground. But an important manifestation of this contraction of interest must surely be seen in the efforts of the early Wittgenstein to plot the limits of language; to draw the boundary between what could be said and what could not, between what could be thought and known and what could not. In brief, he believed that language could express scientific and mathematical propositions and that was all. It was impossible to speak intelligibly or to think about ethics, aesthetics or religion. These lay outside the boundary he had drawn and were what he called 'the mystical'.

Following Wittgenstein, A. J. Ayer and the logical positivists contended that the field of respectable knowledge was now narrowed to include only those truths which could be expressed in scientific language and tested experimentally. Problems of morals, aesthetics and religion – the 'problems of life' with which novelists and poets are concerned – were classified as unreal or as pseudo-problems. In *Language Truth and Logic*, for example, Ayer claims that the propositions of ethics are neither true nor false but simply nonsensical.[1] Sentences which seem to express moral judgements do no more than express the feelings of the person who utters them. Thus, to say murder is wrong is to say no more than that I feel badly when I see or imagine someone being murdered. To claim therefore that Lawrence was a better or more serious writer than other popular novelists of his day, is to do no more than to indicate a prejudice like a preference for red rather than white wine.

And so the scope of rational inquiry was dwarfed and the subsequent retreat by philosophers from the wider fields of our cultural life has been one of the most destructive legacies of the positivist and rationalist spirit. Nietzsche's conception of the philosopher as a critic of culture with the breadth of interest and responsibility which this implies would meet with little sympathy or understanding among English philosophers today. The results of this were appalling; literature, education and political life became impoverished, and philosophy, cut off from its life sources, all but dried up. In 1923 Lawrence lamented this split between fiction and philosophy and he is a tireless critic of the philistinism which results.

He believed that the novel had an important role to play in the critique of this rationalist spirit. It was only in the novel, he thought, that the disembodied thinking mind could be reinserted within the stream of life. For where philosophy tended to present a part of man, the novel would restore his integrity.

This is his point in a short essay called 'Why the Novel Matters'. The parson, the scientist, the philosopher and 'the stupid person' all give us a piece of man and present it as though it was the whole; the novel gives us the total man. The philosopher because he is struck by the importance of thinking decides that only thinking is important and gives us man the thinker and nothing else besides.[2] For this reason Plato can make the ideal being in us tingle but he affects only a part of the whole man in us. In the *Dialogues*, Lawrence says, someone should give Socrates a kick in the wind to show that he is not pure intellect. In the *Timaeus* if someone had interrupted Socrates to say he had a belly-ache and must retire to the privy then we never need have fallen as low as Freud.[3]

This is unfair both to Freud and to Plato. The mistake with Plato derives from Lawrence's attempt to read the *Dialogues* as 'queer little novels' and his failure here to register the fact that the methods and intentions of the philosopher are quite different from those of the novelist. For just as Plato's methods could never have produced *The Rainbow* so the methods of the novelist could never produce those dialogues which make Lawrence's ideal self tingle.

Nevertheless we can see what Lawrence means and can see it illustrated in his own novels. In *Women in Love* Ursula frequently gives Birkin that kick in the wind and as readers we are relieved. But then Birkin is not Plato. And if he did produce a piece of philosophical analysis of the character and style of a Platonic dialogue, the reader's attention would be so changed, the type of response demanded of him so different, that it is difficult to see how the novel as novel could proceed. This merely underlines the fact that the philosopher brings a quite different kind of attention to the reading of his texts from that brought by the writer of fiction.

However Lawrence's quarrel with Plato goes deeper. For him, as for Nietzsche, Plato is not just a philosopher, but a philosopher who is also the embodiment of rationalism and dualism. He is a philosopher for whom 'pure spirit' and 'ideal being' are all-important and a philosopher who teaches us to view the body, its feelings and emotions with a grave distrust. It is not simply Plato as philosopher whom Lawrence attacks but the spirit of rationalism he finds in him which attempts to substitute a part of man for the whole.

But the difficulty does not end here. For Lawrence speaks not just of Plato but of philosophy and the philosopher. Did he think all philosophers were rationalists and does he belong to that group of writers and critics mentioned earlier who think that the philosopher's work is pernicious, especially when it trespasses on those domains which properly belong to the novelist and the poet? Did he not recognize as philosophers thinkers like Nietzsche, who is as determined a critic of rationalism as Lawrence himself?

His position here is ambiguous. For some philosophers, Heraclitus for instance, he expresses an admiration which borders on reverence and elsewhere he claims that art is utterly dependent on philosophy.[4] Nevertheless he is always suspicious of any attempt to produce an adequate account of man outside the novel and here he thinks philosophers have been at fault. Among the culprits he lists Kant, Spinoza, Aristotle and St Thomas Aquinas. Like Nietzsche before him he is particularly hard on that 'beastly Kant'. But they were all at fault in carving up a little piece of human nature and presenting it to the world as the whole. Now Lawrence believes that man does have a nature, that he does maintain a certain integrity which forms the ground of his moral being, but it can never be *directly* expressed as philosophers and moralists have attempted to express it.

> In all this change I maintain a certain integrity. But woe betide me if I try to put my finger on it. If I say of myself, I am this, I am that. – then if I stick to it, I turn into a stupid fixed thing like a lamp-post.[5]

Some philosophers have attempted to identify the self with the ego but in doing this they have merely set up a little ideal and have tried to form themselves in its image. The essential nature of man is mysterious and beyond any attempt to grasp it conceptually.

This view of the self as inexpressible bears an uncanny resemblance to the view of the self outlined by Wittgenstein in his early book *Tractatus Logico-philosophicus*. Here he argues that there are things which cannot be expressed in language. The self, or what he calls 'the metaphysical subject', is just such an entity; it cannot be directly expressed *in* language though it manifests itself *through* language.

This is a difficult notion and Wittgenstein tried to explain it with an analogy of the eye and the field of vision. He thought of the self like the eye and the field of our language and knowledge like the visual field which the eye sees. In the visual field everything can be seen except the eye itself; though if it were not there nothing could be seen at all. It is the limit of the visual field, not a part of it. So the self is not something objective which psychology might study and describe; it is 'rather the metaphysical subject, the limit of the world – not a part of it'.[6] And for this reason Wittgenstein, like Lawrence, believes that there can be no direct expression in language of the self because the limits of the objective world are also the limits of language.

Just how the self is manifest at the limits of language and yet cannot be expressed in language remains a bit of a puzzle and Russell's remark at the time that Mr Wittgenstein seemed to say a great deal about what cannot be said, has still some point. Wittgenstein seems to have thought that in my life I manifest the self from which or towards which I act but that I can never picture this in words which might become the plan or the blueprint for further action. Now here Lawrence thinks the novel has the advantage over philosophy because it never seeks such a blueprint; it depicts only what is within the visual field and permits the self to become manifest there. And indeed it is when the novelist intrudes as moralist in his own novel, telling the reader what to think, what ideal to pursue; it is then, Lawrence thinks, that he betrays his art.

Thus both Lawrence and Wittgenstein are agreed that an abstract or scientific account of the self is impossible; Lawrence because he thinks that such an account would render it a 'stupid fixed thing like a lamp-post' and Wittgenstein because he believes that language can only express the propositions of science or mathematics. Both men, I believe, are wrong; though each in making his mistake has illuminated aspects of our experience of the self which are of real importance. Lawrence, I think, has an unnecessarily restricted view of how philosophy might express its vision of the self as the source of moral propositions while Wittgenstein has an unduly limited notion of the way language works. That Lawrence is wrong does not matter much for he is not a philosopher; it is as a novelist and critic that we value him. And the story of how Wittgenstein came to rethink his own theory of language to become his own sternest critic is now familiar. I will examine these changes later but it will suffice to note here that he came to see how science had worked a spell on him, as it had on so many of his generation, and that he had been wrong to see in the language of science a model for all language. The sources of our language are richer and more diverse than a simple scientific model suggests. Science is simply one form of language among countless others whose uses are as diverse and subtle as the forms of life in which they are found.

The view of man, therefore, which appears in his posthumous *Philosophical Investigations* is never final or nailed down; his open-endedness is one of his essential characteristics and part of the complexity of Wittgenstein's later philosophy springs from the tension he maintains between a notion of the self as something given but at the same time an experiment or project. This is because man creates himself through language which is, at once, something given and handed down but, at the same time, the unique creation of everyone who uses it. The paradox of language is the paradox of the self.

The view of the self which emerges from the major novels of Lawrence will form the subject matter of the subsequent pages. But first, to find a framework from which to work, I want to look at his most sustained and coherent statement of his philosophy of man outside his fiction, that is, in his *Studies in Classic American Literature*.

2 The Theoretical Framework: *Studies in Classic American Literature*

Though a short book, *Studies in Classic American Literature* was an important one for Lawrence. He said that it was the result of five years' persistent work and that it contained a whole *Weltanschauung*.[1] And indeed, studied as a whole, it does give us the clearest statement of his 'metaphysics'.

As we might expect from his discussion of the novel and philosophy and the horror he expressed there at the idea of having things nailed down, there is a great linguistic flexibility in his discussion of the self in this book. His language is often suggestive rather than descriptive in its attempt to avoid classifying and so killing the idea of human integrity. Sometimes he will speak of the 'soul', sometimes 'the self', sometimes 'integrity', sometimes 'nature' and sometimes even 'the Holy Ghost'. And none of these words is used univocally. Sometimes soul means the total integrated human being and at others it means the separated intellectual principle.

The book begins with a question. What was the American artist and what self was he seeking in his departure from Europe? The old answer is, of course, a self which should be free; free from the institutions of European society, from both Church and State and from the identity which these imposed upon the individual. He wanted a new life which meant a new identity and ultimately a new soul. In *Studies* Lawrence examines the evolution of that soul in literature of the eighteenth and nineteenth centuries.

The Americans were right in stressing the importance of freedom but wrong in their understanding of what that concept implied. They failed, Lawrence thinks, to see just how much of the old European self they carried with them to the New World and they gravely misunderstood the extent to which the self is determined by the natural and social environment in which it flourishes.

6

The attitude of the American was negative and therefore he could never achieve real freedom. He sought to flee the old European master but that master was deeply embedded in his own consciousness so that in reality he was in flight from himself and for this reason no American is ever really free. He is in rebellion against the old European parenthood or he is obedient to it, but he cannot escape it and he will always define himself in relation to it.[2] His cries of freedom are merely the rattle of his chains.

Some might find it unusual to see Lawrence stressing the social dimensions of the self and odd to hear him accusing the Americans of neglecting it. For does he not frequently define authentic selfhood in opposition to society? And is there not a stream of Lawrentian characters who find their salvation in departures from Europe and in relationships with Italian peasants or American Indians? This view of Lawrence is simplistic and I will examine it in more detail later. But at least it is clear that here, in *Studies*, he has a sure, if finally undeveloped, grasp of the importance of society in the creation of an authentic individual. Positive freedom, he tells us, depends upon man's place in 'a living, organic, believing community'.[3]

The self cannot be properly constituted in isolation, in 'any escape to some wild west' – nor, we might add, to rural Italy, nor Australia, nor Mexico, and the idea of the noble savage is the product of an enfeebled Romantic imagination. Such a view contains the germ of a social and political philosophy which Lawrence never developed. For if the soul is as dependent upon society as he here claims that it is, then the quest for human integrity cannot be divorced from the creation of the social and political structures which would make such integrity possible.

However, here and elsewhere Lawrence expresses a very different view of the self and one which appears to be at variance with this. For often, he claims, the self which tries to come to terms with society perverts its natural goodness. Ursula Brangwen finds herself in just such a predicament when she tries to perform her duties as a school mistress in order to find her place in the social order. Her spontaneity and her individuality are stifled by a society which will not tolerate an individual who fails to fit the mould it has determined for her. Social life, it would seem, is inimical to personal authenticity.

Is there a way in which these two views can be reconciled? Can the self be seen on the one hand as dependent upon its social relations and on the other as a natural entity more often than not frustrated and destroyed by the social milieu into which it is thrown?

Lawrence's resolution of this dilemma is more complex than it has often been represented but the details of it will only emerge in a study of his major fiction. The broad outlines are, however, sketched here. He views the natural self as a residual concept. It defines certain boundaries within which countless possible selves may be realized. This natural self, which he sometimes calls the Holy Ghost, is unknown in any conceptual way but it nevertheless furnishes an ultimate criterion of value. The man who wilfully crosses these boundaries does violence to his own nature and commits the sin against the Holy Ghost. But human nature can do nothing by itself and it will lie dormant until it begins to create itself in a 'living, organic, *believing* community'. The final result will be a product of both nature and culture.

For Lawrence one of the most daunting aspects of modern thought was its rejection of the concept of human nature. For it is true, that since Hegel declared that the nature of man was an *historical* problem, increasingly the concept of nature receded till it came to be felt that there was nothing in man which might not be changed by a change in his social and economic relations. Against this view he argues that there is a human nature which can provide the basis for judging the kind of self which any society might strive to create. He is consistently opposed to the view that man or society, by an act of choice, can determine the future of man and he could never have accepted the view of Sartre that there is no such thing as human nature and that each man invents his own in his freely chosen projects. It is the *hubris* involved in this extravagant notion of freedom which he exposes in his essay on Poe.

Lawrence, therefore, has a close affinity to natural law philosophers like Aristotle. Aristotle's major error, of course, was to assume that he could see in the ideal fourth-century Athenian citizen the ideal nature of man. Hence he thought he could prescribe in some detail what the 'function' of man was. Lawrence is more timid and with his wider knowledge of different societies is more aware of the complex relationships which exist between nature and culture and so he is loath to make prescriptions. He will never say, 'This is the function of man and this is how everyone must behave.' For in doing this he would merely reproduce the old nailed down self of the moralists which he finds so unliberating. On the other hand, he is not prepared like Sartre to abandon the idea of nature entirely. For although there is no blueprint which can map out all possible roads to fulfilment, there is a human nature and because of it there are certain things a man must not do either to himself or to others. The road is open but there are also *cul-de-sacs*. Many of these appear in Lawrence's novels and can be seen clearly in the characters who are found in them: Miriam, Skrebensky, Hermione, Gerald, etc. But the individuals alone are not at fault. Society can create moral *cul-de-sacs*. Hence the rejection – though never final – of England and later of Italy, Sicily, Australia and Mexico.

In the essay on Benjamin Franklin, Lawrence claims that Franklin's error was to assume that he could provide a complete definition of man and hence a blueprint which everyone could follow. Franklin knew what the perfectibility of man was and he provided a set of rules to which everyone who wanted to achieve that perfection must conform. He, therefore, postulated a fixed nature in man which determines his fulfilment.

Here Lawrence reduces the problem to a simple dichotomy: I can perfect my ideal self as defined by Franklin or I can abandon the protection of his maxims and leave room for the development of 'my wholeness and my dark forest and my freedom'.[4] Lawrence thinks that, rather as Aristotle had presented an ideal fourth-century Athenian citizen as the ideal man, so Franklin carved up the totality of human nature and gave us a respectable eighteenth-century American gentleman as the ideally developed human self.

But man is always more than any such idealized conception suggests:

The *wholeness* of man is his soul. Not merely that nice little comfortable bit which Benjamin marks out . . . . Why, the soul of man is a vast forest, and all Benjamin intended was a neat back garden.[5]

A part of what Lawrence is saying here is already familiar from 'Why the Novel Matters'. For he is viewing Franklin as a paradigm of the anti-novelist who is attempting to nail down the self. The point there was that while there is an integrity or soul it can never be given direct conceptual expression. But here the emphasis is on knowledge rather than its expression. The self cannot be expressed because it cannot be *known* in the first place. The soul is a dark forest and what I know about it can never be more than a clearing in the forest – Franklin's neat back garden.

But there is a paradox and a danger here. The danger, I think, is that which worried T. S. Eliot when he attacked Lawrence in *After Strange Gods*, claiming that he had propounded the most dangerous doctrine ever given to mankind: that everyone should follow his own inner light. Such a doctrine, Eliot believed, led to anarchy and barbarism.

There is certainly point to Eliot's criticism but there are also distinctions which need to be made before it can be applied to Lawrence. Enshrined in the twin concepts of the dark forest and the blood-consciousness is an important antidote to the arrogance of scientific rationalism. For in employing these concepts Lawrence is insisting that man cannot be seen simply as an object of scientific study like other objects. In this Lawrence allies himself to those contemporary philosophers who have fought to expose the limits of scientific investigation and scientific knowledge especially when these are turned on man. The most important of these philosophers is Kierkegaard, the father of existentialism.

Nevertheless there remains the danger that once the criteria of human action are placed beyond reason they are also placed beyond judgement and accountability. It is difficult to see the difference between having unknown criteria and having no criteria at all. And this is why thinkers like Lawrence and Kierkegaard, who have underlined the limits of rational speculation and who in their different ways have sought the clue to the meaning of human experience on the other side of those limits, are so attractive to the fanatical and so easily confused with them.

Therefore Russell's criticism of Lawrence focuses on the irrationality of the blood-consciousness and he claims that Lawrence 'had developed the whole philosophy of fascism before the politicians had thought of it'; that the theory of the blood-consciousness 'led straight to Auschwitz' and that the madness which preceded the Second World War had sprung from just such a sacrifice of reason.

> The world between the wars was attracted to madness. Of this attraction Nazism was the most emphatic expression. Lawrence was a suitable exponent of this cult of insanity.[6]

Kierkegaard was completely unabashed by this paradox and indeed he throws all the resources of his subtle intelligence into sharpening it in his long meditation on the story of Abraham and Isaac. Abraham's decision to kill Isaac is wholly inaccessible to reason; he can explain himself to no one and so he is accountable to no one. He acts by virtue of faith and 'to him who follows the narrow way of faith no one can give counsel, him no one can understand'.[7] Both Lawrence and Kierkegaard viewed with dismay attempts by philosophers to subdue the whole of human life to rationalist principles and both tried to confine these activities within boundaries. On the other side of these boundaries Kierkegaard found faith and Lawrence the blood-consciousness and the dark forest. But in this sacrifice of reason both ran the risk of slipping into fanaticism and if they themselves resisted this tendency there were others who came after them who did not. When the faculty of judgement is jettisoned it is impossible to tell super-reason from sub-reason or super-sense from nonsense.

This is the danger but it should not blind us to the importance of the stand which Lawrence is taking and to its superiority over the brittle intellectualism of Russell, who is his critic. What, then, can be salvaged from Lawrence's position? What he has to say amounts to this: I must act from my whole self but my known self is only a part of this totality. In other words, there is an area of the self which can be known and an area which cannot. Now the difficulty of speaking in this way was noted by Wittgenstein in the preface to his *Tractatus*:

> . . . in order to be able to set a limit to thought, we should have to find both sides of the limit thinkable (i. e. we should have to be able to think what cannot be thought).[8]

Lawrence, in other words, by indicating an area of the self as 'unknown' is already displaying *some* knowledge of it. Indeed the rest of *Studies* is an attempt to express a fuller 'knowledge' of this 'unknown' self. But, as Wittgenstein's remark suggests, this is implicit in the initial position. To declare an area of the self unknown is to express a certain knowledge of it. The force of the paradox is broken when we notice that the word 'knowledge' does not have a univocal sense. There are different kinds of knowledge and a thing which is unknown in one sense can be known in another. The problem arises (and we have Wittgenstein again to thank for this insight) when we become mesmerized by *one* sense of the word 'knowledge' and this is usually the sense of the scientist and the mathematician. We have, as Wittgenstein explains, an irresistible preoccupation with the method of science to the extent that we become frightened to use the word 'knowledge' of anything which is not scientific knowledge.

So, when Lawrence speaks of the unknown self he is defining an area of self-awareness (self-knowledge) which remains unaccounted for in the basically utilitarian framework of Benjamin Franklin. A point that will appear again and again is that often when Lawrence is attacking philosophical expressions of the self, the real object of his criticism is some form of utilitarianism. Thus Franklin presents a pocket-sized self which can be understood in terms of rewards and punishments and he postulates the immortality of the soul only to show that these rewards or punishments will pursue the individual beyond the grave.

This caricature of human nature creates the attitude to sex expressed in Franklin's maxim on chastity – 'Rarely use venery but for health and offspring, never to dullness, weakness, or the injury of your own or another's peace or reputation'[9] – which Lawrence found so repulsive. The place of sex is crucial in the polemic against utilitarianism. For, either man is a being totally accessible to the methods of science and therefore sexuality is wholly explained in terms of pleasure or sensation (which Lawrence believed reduces all sex to a form of masturbation), or there is something about man which is inaccessible to scientific knowledge – the dark forest – and sex is more than the generation of pleasure in the presence of another person; it is an encounter whose *raison d'être* is the expansion of human consciousness through the living expression of the unknown self. The recurring portrayals of sexual experience in the novels are his attempts to sketch, in the best way he believed possible, the contours of the unknown self. Benjamin Franklin knows of no such dimensions to human nature because his view of the self is dwarfed by the concepts in which he is able to conceive it.

It is a classic case of what Birkin means in *Women in Love* when he speaks of being imprisoned within a false set of concepts. When Ursula is teaching her class about catkins Hermione claims that children are damaged when they are stimulated to consciousness too soon; that knowledge kills all spontaneity and all instinct, and that the development of mind is our very death. To which Birkin replies: 'Not because they have too much mind, but too little. . . . [They are] imprisoned within a limited, false set of concepts.'[10] The expression 'not too much mind, but too little' seems to get it exactly right, though I am not sure it was always Lawrence's way of expressing it. For it opens up the possibility of an enlarged reason which can include the dark forest and at the same time provides a footing which can prevent the slide into total irrationality. As we shall see, Lawrence is continually striving to break the stranglehold of these false sets of concepts by producing in the novels an enlarged experience which itself constitutes the kind of knowledge which transcends them.

We can see then in the essay on Franklin that Lawrence is rejecting two connected views of the self. Firstly, there is the one which belongs to the old Greek theistic tradition in which man is seen as a being created by God with a definite nature – which some thought could be defined – and therefore with a definite purpose or goal which could in turn provide the basis for a moral (natural) law. Then there is the utilitarian view – in many ways a development of the first – making a similar point but seeing pleasure as the goal of human life and so defining the self as a being, orientated towards pleasure. Lawrence's view, based on his experience and on his explorations in the novels, is that neither of these descriptions is adequate. For there is something radically mysterious about the human self which is accounted for in neither theory. This extra dimension he expresses by speaking of the unknown self, the dark forest or the blood-consciousness. The function of these concepts is to indicate an area of human experience which remains unaccounted for in any conceptual apparatus hitherto available.

The third essay in *Studies* is on Hector St John de Crèvecoeur and Lawrence sees him as an artist who gives to Franklin's dummy self its most sympathetic setting. For he places man with his divinely given nature against a natural background which guides and directs him, helping him to a clearer understanding of his purpose. Nature and man together provide the ingredients for an ideal partnership. And so Crèvecoeur paints a picture of the American farmer with his amiable spouse and infant son cooperating with the gentle purposes of Nature. This picture Lawrence finds completely unconvincing, especially when he thinks of Crèvecoeur writing it all from the safety of France. Franklin had given us the pocket-sized human being and now Crèvecoeur gives us a pocket-sized world for this creature to inhabit. Where Franklin had wanted to put the human being in his pocket, Crèvecoeur wants to put Nature in his pocket. Between them they want the whole scheme of things in their pockets.

But the crucial difference between Crèvecoeur and Franklin is that Crèvecoeur is an artist as Franklin is not and the artist in him continually contradicts the moralist. The darker side of Nature appears again and again in his writing as the artist broods upon its violent and destructive manifestations. Nature is not merely the source of illustrations for conventional morality; it spills over and invades a world where the eighteenth-century moralist with his narrow system of ethical concepts flounders.

Here we find Lawrence sketching another boundary around what can be understood. The dark forest of the human soul is only a part of the whole order of Nature which is finally mysterious and radically unintelligible. Therefore the moralist who tries to discern the workings of a benevolent purpose in Nature will be continually frustrated by the violence, the waste and the destruction he sees there. We fail to see the true nature of the self or of the natural world to the extent that we view them through any fixed conceptual apparatus. Just as Aristotle and Franklin saw man interpreted by society and thought they saw natural man, so Crèvecoeur saw Nature similarly interpreted and thought he saw the thing itself. But in the work of Crèvecoeur, because he was an artist, the wilderness showed through. And hence Lawrence believes that Nature does not confirm the pocket-sized picture of the self but rather, truthfully viewed and presented by the artist, it shows to man the same inscrutability he found in the dark forest of his own soul. The unintelligibility of the self is a part of the unintelligibility of Nature and the 'scientific' explanation of man. Science can enumerate and relate phenomena but their meaning and purpose finally elude it.

Lawrence sees in the novels of Fenimore Cooper an attempt to get beyond the dummy self of Franklin. Man, he says, always interprets himself in the light of some ideal. But his ideal can get stuck; it can petrify and then it will stifle the self which has essentially outgrown it. For in weakness and nostalgia man hungers for the self which he finds in old novels, old paintings, old music and old moralities. For the Americans the old self was the European self which they brought with them to the New World and which is enshrined in the maxims of Franklin. But this self, Lawrence thinks, is threatened in the confrontation between the Indian and the European and there a context is created in which it can be reappraised and ultimately sloughed.

It is this confrontation which is the theme of Cooper's *Leatherstocking* novels. The White Man can never really understand the Red Man. Nothing in European culture, in European self-awareness, has prepared him for such an understanding; his norms and criteria are different; his very conception of what it means to be human is different and can scarcely include the Indian. It is on this point that Natty Bumppo is continually reflecting in trying to understand his friendship with Chingachgook. The way of the White Man and the way of the Indian are different; the morality of the White Man and the morality of the Indian are different, suggesting almost that they are two different species. In *The Deerslayer*, as he paddles across the lake with Harry Hurry, he discourses on the relative merits of the paleface and the redskin:

God made us all – white, black, and red – and no doubt had his own wise intentions in colouring us differently. Still, he made us, in the main, much the same in feelin's, though I'll not deny he gave each race its gifts. A white man's gifts are Christianized, while the redskin's are more for the wilderness. Thus it would be a great offence for a white man to scalp the dead, whereas it's a signal vartue in an Indian. Then ag'in, a white man cannot amboosh women and children in war, while a redskin may. 'Tis *cruel* work, I'll allow, but for them it's *lawful* work, while for *us* it would be grievous work.[11]

They are different because the Indian soul was never a factor in the development of the European consciousness. So the White Man and the Red Man stand in stubborn opposition. The European consciousness cannot accommodate the Indian and Cooper's idea of the blood-brother relationship between Natty Bumppo and Chingachgook is, Lawrence thinks, only an instance of wish fulfilment.

But it need not be so, if only the White Man could renounce the little white self to which he clings. For then a great new area of human consciousness would open to him and a deeper level of human relationship will be possible. It was of this that Cooper obscurely dreamed in the tales of Natty Bumppo and Chingachgook.

> A stark, stripped human relationship of two men, deeper than the deeps of sex. Deeper than property, deeper than fatherhood, deeper than marriage, deeper than love.[12]

All our relationships hitherto have been poured into moulds determined by words like 'love', 'marriage' 'sex', etc, but Lawrence is suggesting that there are dimensions of the self which lie even deeper than such language. Cooper's insight here enables Lawrence to reflect critically on the way our relationships are moulded by society's view of the good self. The chief agent in this moulding is the common language of society. This is why he frequently writes of relationships which are deeper than sex, deeper than love, etc. For language is the Trojan horse which carries the values of a society over into our very criticism of it. Therefore, the individual is placed in the paradoxical position where, in resisting the self-image which society imposes on him, he must not resist with a new image expressed in language. For language is a public activity and will carry the very disease he is fighting. He must not, therefore, speak of his fulfilment nor even conceive it in terms like 'love', 'fatherhood', 'marriage'. This is why, as we shall see, in *Women in Love* Birkin will not say he *loves* Ursula; he does not want his future imprisoned within the confines of that word nor will he be stifled by the awful weight of history which it carries.

Hence the individual who would find his true self must find it without the aid of all these old categories, for if he does not, he will be shaped by the old, dead social moulds. Without the help of the old words which man has used to understand himself, he must work for the creation of a new social order. Lawrence sees a promise of this order in the novels of Cooper and he attempts something similar himself in the early pages of

The Rainbow. For neither Tom Brangwen nor Lydia Lensky in the earlier and most intense period of their relationship is proficient in the language of the other, and the relationship develops with a minimum of verbal communication.

Thus for Lawrence the value of Cooper's *Leatherstocking* novels lies in that confrontation between Indian and White Man which begins to erode those restrictions which European culture has imposed upon man and his understanding of himself. They help him to break free from the false set of concepts by which he has interpreted himself; they open a path to the dark forest in the soul and put him once again in contact with the deeper resources of his nature.

The first task, then, which the individual must undertake is critical or disintegrative. He must destroy the old self before a new one can emerge. The images of corruption and dissolution in Lawrence's novels and their connection with the Romantic tradition have been well documented by Colin Clarke in *The River of Dissolution*. It is this disintegrative process which Lawrence discerns in the tales of Poe.

Poe chronicles for us the ghastly process of the disintegration of the white consciousness. Lawrence sees *Ligeia* as the crucial story and in particular the epigram from Joseph Glanvill which recurs like a refrain:

> And the will therein lieth, which dieth not. Who knoweth the mysteries of the will, with its vigour? For God is but a great will pervading all things by nature of its intentness. Man doth not yield himself to the angels, nor unto death utterly, save only through the weakness of his feeble will.[13]

For Ligeia the true self is the will; I am what I choose and Ligeia chooses the twin European ideals of love and consciousness to which she clings in life and with even greater tenacity in death. Her husband tells us that he is astonished at the energy of her struggle with death.

> Words are impotent to convey any just idea of the fierceness of her resistance with which she wrestled with the Shadow: . . . in the intensity of her wild desire for life, – for life – *but* for life – solace and reason were the uttermost of folly.[14]

And in the end he comes to recognize that it is her abandonment to love which is the principle of her wild longing 'for the life which was now fleeing so rapidly away'.

Lawrence is horrified at the assertiveness of will which he finds in this tale rather as Paul Morel is horrified at the tenacity with which his mother clings to life in her last days. His attitude to death, as we shall see, is ambivalent but in the context of *Studies* what he wants us to focus on is the assertive will of Ligeia placed in the service of an ideal conception of the person. But, Lawrence insists, the ideal is not the whole person and we are not the great choosers we think. The ideal must be tested on the touchstone of conscience and to do this each man must be vigilant to the promptings of the Holy Ghost within him. To fail in this is *hubris* and it is Ligeia's tragedy. With her immense learning and gigantic volition she wants to play God; to fashion her nature after her own ideal. She refuses to recognize herself as contingent. She accepts nothing in herself which she has not created, over which she has not complete control. Lawrence, however, maintains that there is a human nature and therefore certain laws not of man's creation. We have seen some of these laws already in his essays on Franklin and Crèvecoeur. A life conceived on utilitarian principles will always be less than human. A life restricted by traditional concepts of marriage, love, parenthood, etc, will be less than human. It is the second of these principles which Ligeia transgresses by forcing her nature to conform to an ideal of spiritual love. But Lawrence condemns all actions based on thought (mental consciousness) because he believed that thinking always produced closed systems which imprison the self. In this he seems to ignore thinkers like Nietzsche who believed that an open texture should be the essential characteristic of a good philosophical system. However, in spite of Lawrence's criticisms of abstract thought, his practice both here and in his other works of non-fiction is to attempt to generate just such a speculative understanding.

Hence, he provides two other characteristics of authentic selfhood. First, each self is individual and isolated, but for its life it needs contact with other selves. It is, as we have seen, both individual and social. These limits must be taken into account in contemplating any possible developments.

Now, the tragedy of Ligeia and the persona of the tale, Lawrence tells us, is Poe's own tragedy. Having enjoyed the ecstasy of spiritual love – i.e. of merging with another person through knowing and being known – she erects this into an ideal; she wants to repeat the sensation again and again and with her gigantic volition to define herself in these terms. In other words, she defines herself as 'a being to know and to be known', a project in which she is finally frustrated because of those dimensions of the self which are essentially unknowable. But it is important to define the kind of knowledge with which Ligeia is concerned. It is analytic and the persona of the tale is continually trying to possess Ligeia by analysing all her component parts. Hence those long passages of description in the tale where he dwells on her voice, her complexion, her nose and above all her eyes, trying all the time to probe the mystery of her and to find that explanation which he can never find. For only what is dead can be dissected and this type of dissection produces a kind of psychic death.

Therefore Lawrence claims that Poe is more of a scientist than an artist and it is the *kind* of knowledge which Poe pursues that he finds so destructive. Hence his comments here do not preclude, in fact they imply, another kind of knowledge by which the dark forest of the human soul can respectfully be apprehended. It is that kind of knowledge which Lawrence expressed in the poem 'She Said as Well to Me'; the kind which makes me hesitate as I approach the dark forest of another's soul. But Lawrence is too easily inclined to sacrifice the word 'knowledge' to the scientists and consequently he develops the disastrous dualism implied in the notion of the 'blood-consciousness'.

It is a tragic consequence of Lawrence's failure to analyse more fully the concept of knowledge that, although instinctively a great critic of dualism, he created a conceptual apparatus which reintroduced an inverted form of it. Much of his criticism was directed against the Neoplatonic tradition which identified the self with the spiritual element in man and devalued the importance of the body and the emotions. Much of what he has to say about sex is best understood as an attack on dualism; man's sexual activity must not be seen as something merely physical; on the contrary it is an extended dimension of his essential nature. Hence his jibe that the Pope knows more about sex than G. B. Shaw because he knows more about the essential nature of the human person, having a thousand years' experience![15]

But the essential integrity of the human person is threatened by Lawrence himself when, in the essay on Nathaniel Hawthorne, he speaks of the blood-consciousness and the mind-consciousness and claims that there is a deep hatred between the two. As evidence of this he tells us that cultured people hate washing dishes and that his own father hated books.[16] It is this kind of slovenly thought and the language it produces which led him to suggest in 1916 that a man might need two wives, one for his blood-consciousness and another to satisfy his mental-consciousness. The concept of the two consciousnesses makes the integrity of the self impossible and implies that in man the source of action must fluctuate from one to the other.

Dimmesdale in Hawthorne's novel *The Scarlet Letter* embodies the spiritual consciousness. This, as we have seen, is a form of Neoplatonism. But Lawrence rightly sees that this is not an historical phenomenon which can be labelled and forgotten; it is not just a problem for academics. No, it is a dangerous flaw in contemporary culture. For in our times mind-consciousness has become dominant and many people who never heard the name of Plato are caught firmly in his grip. The dialogue with Plato, for Lawrence as for Nietzsche, is a matter of immediate contemporary relevance and cannot be evaded by having it assigned, as some contemporary British philosophers would like, to the mere 'history of philosophy'.

Although Lawrence is generally opposed to the identification of the self with the spiritual consciousness, he nevertheless admits that Dimmesdale achieves a certain integrity while he acts sincerely from that view of himself in which he genuinely believes. He achieves that moral integrity which every man can achieve by acting authentically from what he believes, even when he is mistaken. Paradoxically, it is when Dimmesdale begins to act from a more physical conception of himself that Lawrence believes he loses his integrity. When he allows Hester to seduce him, he falls.

Now, working from Lawrence's usual priorities, we might expect Dimmesdale to find his salvation here because he is acting for the first time from his solar plexus and in defiance of his mental consciousness. Does not Mellors save Connie Chatterley from the brittle intellectualism of Clifford's world by causing her to act from the deeper physical reserves of her nature? But there is a difference. Connie believes in what she is doing and so she preserves the integrity of her belief and her feelings; Dimmesdale does not believe in what he is doing and his psyche is split in two. He destroys the only self of which he is capable. True, it was a thinking, intellectual self, but it was the best he could do and it was a unity. For Lawrence a man must stick to the belief in which he is grounded, or completely abandon that belief and prepare himself for a new one. Dimmesdale prevaricates between the two and is lost. He should never have surrendered to Hester until he had discarded the old spiritual idea of the self and replaced it with a larger idea which included the blood-consciousness.

In this Lawrence is making two important points about the self. Firstly, each man must act honestly from whatever principle he is grounded on. Then he can act with integrity even when he is wrong. For in this he attains that peculiar moral integrity which derives its worth not from 'what it effects because of its fitness for achieving some proposed end', as Kant expressed it, but rather 'through its willing alone'.[17] Thus, for Lawrence, Dimmesdale is a man who, although objectively mistaken in identifying himself with his spiritual consciousness alone, might have achieved that moral integrity had he stuck to that belief and acted upon it. Miriam in Lawrence's own *Sons and Lovers* finds herself in a similar predicament.

However, doing what we believe is not enough. Each man must be concerned at the adequacy of his beliefs to the reality they seek to express and interpret. This, as we have seen, is what separates Lawrence from Sartre. For Sartre I create my reality from my choices and actions, while for Lawrence I possess a given reality to which I must ever make more sensitive adjustments. It follows from this that to act from a mistaken concept of the self always puts a strain on my capacity to act authentically, because that part of myself which the false concept excludes will continue to seek its satisfaction. Hence Dimmesdale. His idealized view of himself denied the importance of the body, but the body would not be denied.

Women, then, make fools of spiritual men and sex becomes the crucible in which a man's concept of the self is put to the test. For the blood-consciousness will always be active where there is real sexual contact and a spiritual relationship between a man and woman based on their two 'known' selves will always be threatened. And so woman is the nemesis of doubting man because she appeals beyond the cosy concept he has of himself as a spiritual being to the dark forest in his soul; his belief in a merely spiritual self is undermined. Hester, and later her daughter, Pearl, are two such destructive women.

But we must be careful, for Lawrence's language is ambivalent here. When he says they are both demonical he does not mean that they are so to him, but only to those, like Dimmesdale, who wish to preserve the old, false, European consciousness and the morality which sustains it. And therefore in our on-going struggle into consciousness, evil is as necessary as good. Like Nietzsche, he feels the need to transcend the criteria of good and evil based on the old European concept of the self. Good and evil are both necessary and therefore in a higher sense *good* for the growth of a new self more sensitively adjusted to those unknown dimensions of human nature.

The spirituality of Dimmesdale's Christianity, the utilitarianism of Franklin and the existentialism of Sartre, are all united in showing a lack of reverence for the body and hence, for Lawrence, they diminish a whole dimension of human nature. They all see the body as purely instrumental. For the Christian dualist it is something to be subdued; for the utilitarian it is merely the source of sensations; while for Sartre it is given its meaning and significance from the decisions of consciousness.

What Lawrence seeks to establish through his analysis of Dimmesdale, and otherwise in his fiction, is that the body is not merely an instrument of the soul but a constitutive part of it; through it the blood-consciousness asserts itself, not just as a device at the service of mind, but as a part of the very structure of human consciousness.

But is Lawrence, then, committed to an inverted dualism? In stressing the importance of blood over intellect is he perpetuating and reinforcing the very split in human experience against which he was reacting? Certainly his language does not always do justice to the unity of human experience; to that mental knowledge which is an integral part of emotional experience, indeed, to the extent to which emotions cannot be characterized apart from their cognitive content. Nevertheless he does indicate a principle of unity. It is true that man loses his integrity when he acts from a principle in which he does not believe. He should never do what he believes to be wrong. But if the sources of his actions are dual – from the blood and the mind – and if these principles are most of the time in opposition to one another, [18] then it is inevitable that his actions will be disbelieved in by one part of his nature. Therefore he will continually be acting against what one part of himself believes. But this is not what Lawrence is saying. The real self is to be identified with neither principle. For there is a third principle which lies deeper than either blood or mind; it is a unifying principle which enables us to discriminate, which tells us when to choose the blood and when to choose the mind. He calls it the Holy Ghost.

Bertrand Russell, therefore, is mistaken in speaking of Lawrence's mystical philosophy of the blood, when he implies that Lawrence was preaching a complete surrender to the blood-consciousness. On the other hand, Lawrence's insistence on the separation and total independence of the two seats of consciousness was bound to generate confusion, especially when he insists that a choice must be made between them. Furthermore, in his efforts to redress what he saw as the excessive importance given in his time to the mind – and here Russell was one of the chief offenders – he does tend to place undue emphasis on the 'irrational'. But here he must be seen as trying to correct an imbalance, so that his non-fiction, and at times even his fiction, is polemical. He knew that in a different climate different things would need to be stressed.

In R. H. Dana's *Two Years Before the Mast* Lawrence finds an honest record of the connections between the individual human being and the physical universe. This is important for him because he believes that the two can never really be separated. This is always the consequence of a rejection of dualism. While man is identified with his spiritual being, then his body and the physical universe are extrinsic to his real nature. But once we reject this split and see him as a totality we begin to become aware of the extent to which the material universe influences him and indeed is a part of the permanent structure of his being. Hence the great Christian critic of dualism, Teilhard de Chardin, writes:

> We live at the centre of a network of cosmic influences. . . . It is worthwhile performing the salutary exercise which consists in starting with those elements of our conscious life in which our awareness of ourselves as persons is most fully developed, and moving out from there to consider the spread of our being. We shall be astonished at the extent and the intimacy of our relationship with the universe.[19]

It is this spread of our being that Lawrence finds in Dana. The sea is more than the background against which his tale develops; it becomes constitutive of the conscious life of his characters. *Two Years Before the Mast* is the story of a man's battle with the sea, not only a physical battle, but an inward battle of the soul. Its hero is confronted by chaos, by a reality which spills over all mental categories, and which he fights to include within his own conscious life. Dana comes out victorious but not before the sea tortures his living, integral body. The book is an experience in the extension of human consciousness, which, Lawrence declares elsewhere, is the purpose of human life and the meaning of work.[20] It engenders that understanding which grows and grows until we realize that there is something we can never understand. This extension of human consciousness and the new understanding it entails reintroduces the now familiar paradox which plays upon the distinction between knowledge understood in its narrow scientific sense and that enlarged experience which so much of his fiction was able to create.

Lawrence's rejection of merely mental knowledge has reinforced the view that he was advocating a return to instinctual life. Furthermore, there are things in his work which give credence to this view. There is his fascination with the Etruscans, with the Indians and, in England, with gypsies and gamekeepers. T. S. Eliot was horrified at Connie Chatterley's desire to give herself to 'a plebeian' and at those other heroines who 'sought out savages'![21] Then there are his own wanderings in rural Italy, Sicily and Mexico. In other words, there is much to suggest that he is turning his mind towards primitive peoples and primitive societies hoping to find there some alternative to the *cul-de-sac* into which our modern culture has condemned us. It is true that he thought he could discern hints and clues among primitive peoples which helped him to define more clearly the sickness he detected in contemporary civilized life. This is particularly true of his studies of the Etruscans. However, his claim that the purpose of human life is the extension of human consciousness should alert us to the fallacy in this view.

For in the essay on Melville he allies himself with Melville's own rejection of the merely primitive. For Melville too was attracted by the idea of the noble savage but in the end found it wholly inadequate. He had the same contempt for much that he saw in modern life. He hated our human life, Lawrence tells us, and at the same time was filled with a sense of the immensity and the enigma of that life which was not human; he was impelled to try to see over our horizons. This is why Lawrence sees Melville as one of his great precursors, for the need to enlarge our concept of life beyond the 'merely human' is a constant theme with Lawrence.

Of course the notion 'human life' is ambiguous. When Lawrence speaks of 'our human life' he means that life which is confined within those categories by which man has hitherto understood himself. Hence, when Melville tries to see over the horizon, he is breaking the shell of the old self so a new one can begin to be born. What the Indians were to Cooper, the South Sea Islanders are to Melville; a people whose culture and identity were formed in complete innocence of the Old Europe. So among these islanders Melville hoped to get a perspective on humanity which owed nothing to those aspects of European culture which he hated. In part he achieved this but what he saw was a disappointment to him. For he found there a people scarcely created; to become like them would involve a regression in conscious life which was neither possible nor desirable. Lawrence himself had been subject to these temptations and like Melville had recognized their futility. He now knows, he tells us, that there can be no going back.[22] For a regression to the uncreated life of the savage would be the very antithesis of his definition of the purpose of human life as the extension of consciousness. Therefore, although like Melville he had a great distaste for much of what he saw in modern 'civilized' living, he recognizes that in living through all those centuries of civilization and the experiences which that entailed, we have been living forward and the future lies with the civilized world. Thus, in spite of occasional flirtations with more primitive forms of life, his experiences in Italy, Mexico, etc, and the norms built into his conception of the self, prevent him finally from advocating any simple solution. In a letter of 1922 speaking of the Indians of Taos and saying that we have to continue to go ahead, continue forward, he says, 'We can go back and pick up some threads, but these Indians are up against a dead wall more than we are.'[23]

Consequently his interest in primitive peoples must be seen as this picking up of threads and nothing more. For he recognizes that a purely natural, inchoate self, uninfluenced by language or society, is not a reality and certainly not a goal worth striving after; the self is a product of nature and society. His fears are centred on society's tendency to inhibit future developments by petrifying, in a conceptual framework, some earlier stage of growth. Melville is important because in his excursions into 'non-human' forms of life he reopens possibilities which civilized life had closed.

Moby Dick is that non-human life and Ahab's monomania the last effort of the mental consciousness to subdue and destroy it. In Ahab we see the hatred and fear which civilized man has for that life he can neither subdue nor understand. When Starbuck accuses him of madness to be so enraged with a dumb thing, Ahab replies:

All visible objects, man, are but as pasteboard masks. But in each event – in the living act, the unbounded deed – there, some unknown but still reasoning thing puts forth the mouldings of its features from behind the unreasoning mask. If man will strike, strike through the mask. . . . I see in him outrageous strength, with an inscrutable malice sinewing it. That inscrutable thing is chiefly what I hate; and be the white whale agent or be the white whale principal, I will wreak that hate upon him. Talk not to me of blasphemy, man. I'd strike the sun if it insulted me.[24]

But of course it is blasphemy and as such Lawrence understands it.

The ambiguities of American fiction arise out of the conflict between two different concepts of man and of the two moralities to which these gave birth. This is the morality of the author and the morality of the tale. The author's morality is the old morality according to which the soul is superior to the body. To this morality the American gives a tight intellectual allegiance. But against the author's conscious intention, the morality of the tale rebels and is bent on the destruction of the old spiritual morality.

Walt Whitman is the first American to put an end to this conflict between soul and body by locating the soul *in* the body. That moral prerogative which the mind, identified with the 'soul', achieved over the body is gone and the soul once more becomes the *anima* of the body – 'the first principle of life in livings things', to use the old formula of

Aristotle. Whitman divests the soul of its thin spirituality and plants it firmly in the flesh, in the limbs, in the lips and in the belly.[25]

Lawrence admires Whitman because of his determination to take the body seriously but what he does not know is that a similar service was performed in Europe by Nietzsche. For in his attack on Platonism, which is one of the central themes of his *Twilight of the Idols*, Nietzsche, though a philosopher himself, sets out to give the body its place. Speaking of German culture he tells us that to discipline our thoughts and feelings is not sufficient; we must start with the body and

> inaugurate culture in the *right place* – not in the soul (as has been the fateful superstition of priests and quasi-priests): the right place is the body, demeanour, diet, physiology: the *rest* follows.[26]

Nietzsche and Lawrence are united in their dismay at the ways in which men become the slaves of ideas; they see how the individual or society can be stultified in their growth by a fixed conception of the self or of right. This is why Lawrence tries to warn of the tyranny words like 'love', 'charity', 'sympathy', can exercise. This is why Nietzsche attacks the whole language of nineteenth-century Christian morality; why he claims the Church has used the concept of sin against man, imprisoning him in a cage whose bars are constructed of nothing but frightening concepts.[27] And this is like Birkin's response to Hermione when he claims that we are becoming imprisoned within false sets of concepts.

Lawrence began these essays by noting the importance which the American artist attached to freedom. In the subsequent essays he tried to show how this freedom was never fully realized, largely because the Americans failed to appreciate how much of the old European master they carried around in their language and in their subconscious minds. In the end, however, he wants to isolate freedom as the chief characteristic of the self but freedom now, as he thinks, properly understood.

Since man's freedom is destroyed by his enslavement to traditional concepts of the self or of right, it can only be restored when he finds the courage to act independently of such concepts. He must not bind himself to any mental concepts whatever; not to the idea of self-sacrifice, nor to the idea of love, nor even to the idea of sex. The future of the self is the Open Road. On the negative side the picture here is like Sartre's. The individual must never subject himself to any extrinsic system of rules. But unlike Sartre, Lawrence insists that he must subject himself to something other than his own freedom. This something is the soul, the Holy Ghost or the dark forest. These expressions, as Lawrence demands, remain obscure. For it is not always an easy thing to distinguish those inspirations which come from the dark forest from more transient impulses deriving from sources in our conscious life which are less fully human. Later in the novels, and more abstractly in *A Propos of Lady Chatterley's Lover*, he will try to distinguish more clearly between our emotions and our deeper emotions, our needs and our deeper needs. In the latter book, for instance, when he is discussing the conflict in man between his desire for fidelity on the one hand and his obvious promiscuous instincts on the other, he says that world-history shows his instinct for fidelity to be just a little deeper – more intrinsic to his essential nature – than his desire for faithless sexual promiscuity. Among other things this shows Lawrence's recognition of the need for a philosophical anthropology.

In *Studies*, then, we have Lawrence's most sustained attempt outside his fiction to express his concept of the self. His most consistently held view, of course, is that the best expression of the self is in the novel; no direct, non-fictional expression is ever adequate. So when he does attempt to discuss the self outside the novels and stories, he leans heavily on metaphor and analogy. Furthermore, in *Studies* he establishes his priorities through his criticism of other novels. This method is also used by Sartre. Some of his most recent philosophical enquiries occur in long critical essays on Baudelaire, Genet and Flaubert. This in itself, Lawrence believes, tells us a good deal about the nature of the self.

Had Lawrence been a better philosopher, or perhaps had his acquaintance with modern philosophers been other than with the arid intellectualism of Russell, he might have been better placed to explore the implications of his own non-fictional picture of the self. He might have realized, too, the possibility of achieving a greater conceptual clarity without descending to the pocket-sized self of Benjamin Franklin.

We shall achieve some of this clarity if in summarizing Lawrence's position we place it alongside the views of an existentialist philosopher like Nietzsche.

Firstly, Lawrence maintains that man must never try to lead his life by reference to any preconceived blueprint such as Franklin provided in his system of maxims. This in itself is a common theme not only with Nietzsche but with many existentialist thinkers. But Lawrence resembles Nietzsche even more closely than this when he draws our attention to the ways in which any attempt to situate the self within a system of concepts can subvert its freedom; in fact anyone who tries to describe the self unavoidably nails it down. Nietzsche in his turn attacks all those philosophers who seek to construct systems or who try to situate themselves within systems:

> The will to *system*: in a philosopher, morally speaking, a subtle corruption, a disease of the character; amorally speaking, his will to appear more stupid than he is. . . . I am not bigoted enough for a system – and not even for my system.[27]

For him philosophical systems are provisional methods in the education of spirit, constantly in need of revision and reinterpretation. Like Lawrence he is aware of the dangers in submitting to any one systematic description of man. This awareness leads Lawrence to suspect every philosophical description of man and to look to the novel, 'the little bright book of life', as an alternative. Nietzsche, on the other hand, accepts the importance of philosophical systems, provided we know how to use them. The philosopher of the future will not be tempted to nail down the self because he will never take any system as final:

> For I treat deep problems as I would a cold swim – Quickly into them and quickly out again. That in this way one does not get deep enough *down*, that is the superstition . . . of the enemies of cold water; they speak without experience.[28]

He will use philosophical systems, so as not to be imposed upon by them. With ruthless consistency he applies this insight to himself and to his own work; his propositions too are tentative. Hence the remark of his Zarathustra:

> One repays a teacher badly if one remains only a pupil . . . .
> Now I bid you lose me and find yourselves; and only when you have denied me will I return to you.[29]

Lurking behind all such remarks by Nietzsche there is a radical scepticism to which Lawrence never subscribed. This is revealed in a fragment from *The Will to Power* where Nietzsche gives his definition of truth as that 'kind of error without which a certain species of life could not survive'.[30] Both men, then, are agreed that philosophy is unable to give us an adequate picture of the nature of man. Lawrence because he thought there was something fundamentally mysterious about human nature and Nietzsche because he thought there was no such thing; it is because man is not a *thing* that there can be no final truth about him. This last point is only hinted at by Nietzsche and he is not always consistent about it. However the idea is developed by Sartre and, for him, indeed, man has no nature; he is his own project and his nature is the creation of his own choices and decisions.

It is at this point that Lawrence parts company with the existentialists. For he believes that we are not the great choosers we think we are; that there is a human nature although it always eludes our efforts to capture it in words. And this is why, in spite of the affinity between them, Lawrence is totally opposed to Nietzsche's conception of 'will to power'.

Further similarities can be seen in their attitudes to Nature. Both are critics of any *simple* Romantic interpretation here for both have a sense of that outrageous strength and inscrutable malice which hides behind the mask. Here Lawrence's criticism of Crèvecoeur is paralleled by Nietzsche's criticism of David Strauss. For Nietzsche Strauss was a naïve nineteenth-century atheist who believed he could let slip the idea of God and still retain the moral order which depended upon that idea. He thought that science could replace religion and that the reverence which the Christian directed towards God could now be directed towards the universe interpreted by science. But Nietzsche follows Schopenhauer here; Strauss's optimism is merely the uneclipsed afterglow of Christianity. If God is dead, the universe is blind and without purpose. After the death of God, Nietzsche maintains, it is absurd to see man or the world as the result of any special design or purpose; the concept of purpose is a human invention. And the universe is a vacant machine and man should take care lest he gets caught in its wheels.

Now Lawrence, as we have seen, follows Nietzsche in rejecting any popularized Romantic interpretation of Nature. But his rejection is based on the belief, not that things are without purpose, but that their purposes are wholly mysterious. Like Ahab he senses in the world some unknown but still reasoning thing. Philosophers have to elucidate this, as they try to explain the nature of man, but here too there is something which eludes them. But it manifests itself in great novels like *Moby Dick*. Nevertheless there is purpose there both in the self and in the larger world, which resists any merely human attempt to reinterpret it. Such a view is not consistent with atheism. Nietzsche is correct here. A world in which we can discern purpose implies an intelligence whose purpose it embodies. So that in spite of the iconoclasm of 1915 and after, Lawrence remains a religious writer to the extent that he never abandoned these views. Thus when in a letter to Russell he says that his Christian religiosity has been muddiness and that he must drop all talk about God, it is not religion as such that he is reacting against but a redundant expression of it.

The views of Nietzsche and Lawrence converge again in their criticism of dualism. Both rejected the idea that the real nature of man is spiritual. Nietzsche believed that the source of this error could be found in Christianity and that Christianity itself was merely a popularized form of Plato's philosophy. Plato thought that the body was the prison of the soul, was evil and that the soul sought release from it, a release partly attained in this life by philosophers and ascetics and finally achieved in death. The Church, therefore, is the enemy of the passions and seeks their extirpation. 'But to attack the passions at their roots means to attack life at its roots: the practice of the Church is hostile to life.'[31] The suspicion with which modern men and women view their passions and the whole of their natural instinctual life is, Nietzsche thought, one of the most mischievous legacies of Christian Platonism. In its place Nietzsche advocates a life which is neither solely spiritual nor solely physical but an integrity of both. What he aspires to is totality and that totality which he thought he saw in the cultured naturalism of Goethe in his last years at Weimar.

Lawrence too believed that the reinstatement of the body to its proper place as a part of our conscious life was a matter of urgent contemporary importance. This is the theme of his essay on the Etruscans. However his position weakens when, from beneath, he introduces a new kind of dualism; when in place of the old dualism of the dominance of the spirit over the body he substitutes the new cult of the body over the spirit.

And finally there is a glint of hope even for those who are mistaken. Even that man who can see no further than the diminutive self of Franklin or the ghostly self of Plato can still maintain his integrity if he acts on what he believes to be true. He will achieve authenticity, though he may not realize the optimum possibilities of his nature.

3 The Rejection of Idealism: *The White Peacock* and *Sons and Lovers*

In Lawrence's first novel, *The White Peacock*, many of the themes from *Studies* are found in seminal form. The protagonists – in particular Lettie and George – are individuals in search of their authentic selves.

The most persistent obstacle in their path is the presence of a mind/body dualism like that discussed in *Studies*. In this novel Lawrence maintains that women are responsible for the perpetuation of this dualism. It is they who embrace the spiritual ideal and propagate it. Lettie, the heroine of the book, in the end chooses a form of life which excludes everything coming from the dark forest. The self she chooses is spiritual or mental and its origins are social.

Nevertheless in the earlier parts of the book she does entertain a view of life which is larger than this and which is embodied in her attraction for George Saxton, the animal; her *taurus*. In the earlier chapters of the novel she is pulled in different directions, sometimes responding to the darker physical life represented by George and at others aspiring to a state of sophistication and culture where she finds him coarse and unworthy. This idealized life is more in keeping with her social expectations and in the end it is to society's pressures that she succumbs, using them as an alibi for her rejection of George. She tells him, in fact, that she cannot help herself, that she has been brought up in a certain way and that certain things are expected of her:

> 'You see, I couldn't help it.'
> 'No, why not?'
> 'Things! I have been brought up to expect it – and you're bound to do what people expect you to do – you can't help it.'

We can't help ourselves, we're all chessmen.[1] We have already seen Lawrence warn of the danger into which the individual falls when he permits society to determine his nature and its goals. For continually, through its morals, its language and its images, society forces an ideal upon the individual which he then attempts to reproduce. But Lettie, in a paradigm of what Sartre calls 'bad faith', extricates herself from the struggle implicit in this description by maintaining that in the end the outcome is inevitable; society must always win.

But what is the nature of the self which society urges Lettie to become? Its positive contours are never clearly defined in the novel because Leslie, the prize of her social aspirations, is himself a shadowy and ill-defined character. However it clearly has something to do with being well-off, with being 'cultured' and with being able to mix with the right people. Later it will come to include the mother image as well. Nevertheless, if its positive contours are blurred, its negative ones are less so. The self which Lettie rejects included that whole area of physical life which George offered. This life becomes increasingly distasteful to her while it remains unredeemed by culture. But her choice is not made easily. She has to fight with her attraction for George, annihilating that part of herself which he keeps alive and which she has chosen to reject. And from her ideal nature she hates him for this and so must continually humiliate him.

She partly succeeds with the ideal self she has chosen by shutting out that part of her nature which she cannot consciously accept. Unlike Dimmesdale in *The Scarlet Letter*, she maintains a certain integrity, albeit a very narrow one; she manages to cocoon herself.

> Like so many women she seemed to live, for the most part contentedly, a small indoor existence with artificial light and padded upholstery. Only occasionally hearing the winds of life outside.[2]

Then, when her ideal of herself as a cultured young woman sours and begins to recede, society is ready to replace it with another ideal self – one which Lawrence was to view with increasing suspicion – that of arrogant motherhood. For motherhood, as it is appropriated here by Lettie and later by Anna Brangwen, is only a further evasion, a further denial of responsibility for the real self. Looking at Lettie, her brother Cyril tells us that he 'longed for a place where . . . young, arrogant, impervious mothers might be a forgotten tradition'.[3] For when the brittle idealism of her youth begins to crumble, Lettie continues to conceal the truth from herself behind her new ideal.

She was at bottom quite sincere. Having reached that point in a woman's career when most, perhaps all of the things in life seemed worthless and insipid, she had determined to put up with it, to ignore her own self, to empty her own potentialities into the vessel of another or others, and to live life at second hand. This particular abnegation of the self is the resource of a woman for the escaping of the responsibilities of her own development. . . . She had now determined to abandon the charge of herself to serve her children.[4]

She has attained that level of maturity where she sees her early ideals as hollow and insipid; a chance for the death of that old self and the birth of a new. But she rejects this newly won freedom and again escapes the responsibility for her own development. She abandons herself to serve her children.

However in this book the theme of motherhood is only touched upon. Probably Lawrence is unable to deal with things which lie so close to the centre of his personal life. The mother of Lettie and Cyril is a remote character and has little influence on the action of the novel. Their father is presented as a vulgar, dishonest person who, after a brief appearance, dies. It is difficult not to see in this a Freudian disclosure of Lawrence's feelings for his own father. For he found Arthur Lawrence coarse and uncultivated and was never able to invest his strong physical life with the charm it has in George Saxton. Lawrence's mother with her 'superior soul' seeking to annihilate that physical life is also the mother of Lettie. But the idea of the arrogant mother has not yet become the centre of Lawrence's creative attention. In *The White Peacock* he is content to note that the ideal of motherhood, like other culturally derived ideals, diverts Lettie from the care for her own development.

But if Lettie achieves a certain wholeness for herself, her idealism completely undermines George. His studies of Schopenhauer, of William James, and rudimentary metaphysics appear to us merely ridiculous. Furthermore, that culture-philistinism accomplished in Lettie, to which he aspires, is little better. Her use of Gounod's 'Ave Maria' as a cheap spell to make him soulful and forgetful of his petty cares;[5] her tirade against him because he cannot share her idealized, romantic view of Nature; her efforts to make him ashamed of his physical passion for her;[6] all combine to undermine him and alienate him from himself. When he sees himself placed beside the world of her ideals, he feels worthless and finds nothing in himself of which he can be proud: '. . . it is rotten', he says, 'to find there isn't a single thing you have to be proud of.'[7]

This dilemma has been remarked by some contemporary educationalists. The anguish of George Saxton when he views himself beside the bogus standards of Lettie's nineteenth-century culture is not unlike that suffered by some Latin American peoples. For they too, as Paulo Freire points out, have come to see themselves as 'marginal men' because they have been taught to judge themselves by the standards of the developed countries. They become 'underprivileged' when they adopt our standards and measure themselves with our gauges, till, like George, they can find very little of which they can be proud.

One difficulty with this book is that the author is partly committed to the values of the cultured middle class which the book itself shows to be so wasteful and destructive. This is a case to follow Lawrence's own advice to distrust the artist and trust the tale. For he himself seems partly bemused by the dummy standards to which Lettie aspires and at times finds it hard himself to say what George has to be proud of. However over the years as Lawrence's insight matured, his grasp of the bankruptcy of what he calls 'idealism' – in whatever disguise it masquerades – grows, so that he succeeds in defining with increasing clarity the values embodied in George Saxton and other characters like him till the possibilities represented by them become almost normative.

In *The White Peacock* Lawrence sees woman as the chief carrier of this false idealism. She must always view life through the categories of romance or religion. Consequently she devalues all those dimensions of experience which her chosen idealism cannot include. This point is made most forcibly by the gamekeeper Anable when he sees in a peacock perched on an angel's head in the churchyard a symbol of woman. The bird screeches and dirties the angel's head. That, he declares, is the soul of woman – vanity and defilement:

> The proud fool! look at it! Perched on an angel, too, as if it were a pedestal for vanity. That's the soul of woman – or it's the devil. . . . Just look . . . the miserable brute has directed the angel. A woman to the end, I tell you, all vanity and screech and defilement.[8]

For, like George, he has been humiliated 'in the pride of his body' by a woman. She is a Lady Crystabel – the name itself is 'poetic' and therefore idealized – who creates her life of images drawn from the most debased forms of romanticism. Some of her notions are derived from a sloppy French novel, called *The Romance of a Poor Young Man*. In ways like this reality is defiled.

It is a form of what Nietzsche called *resentment*; a resentment which creates an ideal world because it finds the real world too distasteful.

Then in turn the real world is found even more repulsive by comparison with the ideal.

> It is suffering that inspires these conclusions: fundamentally they are desires that such a world should exist: in the same way, to imagine another more valuable world is an expression of hatred for a world that makes one suffer; the *resentment* of metaphysicians against reality is here creative.[9]

For Nietzsche, dualism, in whatever form it is found – soul/body, real world/apparent world, this life/the next life – is always a product of resentment and is always destructive. The origin of this resentment, he believes, can be found in Judaeo-Christian culture. The Jews were 'the first to coin the word "world" as a term of infamy'. Christianity is the heir to this resentment and its practice is hostile to life as seen not least in its attitude to death:

> The certain prospect of death could sweeten every life with a precious and fragrant drop of levity – and now you strange apothecary souls have turned it into an ill-tasting drop of poison that makes the whole of life repulsive.[10]

And for him the most recent exponents of these views were priests and philosophers – those of the German idealist tradition in particular.

It is this resentment against reality and the accompanying commitment to idealism that Lawrence finds in Lettie and Christabel. However, he was to identify the source of this sickness differently throughout his life. Sometimes, like Nietzsche, he sees it in the Church and there is a close similarity between Lawrence's last piece of non-fiction, *Apocalypse*, and some of Nietzsche's later works. In his mature works he finds it more often in the culture-Philistines of Bloomsbury and then in the mentality of industrialized capital. Here he maintains that woman is the source of the evil.

The novel, however, does not fully endorse this view. Anable claims that it is the *nature* of woman to be vain, to dirty the heads of angels and to insult the life of the body. But a study of Lettie's conflict does not really support this view. In *Studies* Lawrence had noted that the self was partly a product of Nature and partly a product of society. Now, the social self to which Lettie aspires is unable to encompass the whole richness of her nature. Hence, in attaining it, she is forced to kill some of the best things in herself. She does respond to George, does desire the physical relationship he offers. But the self which possessed these desires has been overlaid by another and stifled. So, in the end, although she chooses that life of sophistication which society expects her to, the choice is made without complete conviction and with the sense that something has been lost. 'Do you think', she asks, 'we can lose things of the earth? . . . I believe I have lost something.' And this something is identified as 'something out of an old religion we have lost'.[11]

Thus we are led to suspect that woman herself is not naturally hostile to reality but rather that there is something about her position in society and with the expectations imposed upon her which makes her so. Cyril, indeed, suggests at one point that George could have evoked a deeper response from her and could have committed her to a fuller development had he possessed the courage for what he really was:

> You should have had the courage to risk yourself – you're always too careful of yourself and your own poor feelings – you never could brace yourself up for a shower-bath of contempt and hard usage, so you've saved your feelings and lost. . . .[12]

Thus Lettie's destructiveness is partly a product of society and partly of George's failure to believe in himself. Woman is the nemesis of doubting man. George is a curious inversion of Arthur Dimmesdale; his spirituality is undermined by Hester because he is hesitant and uncertain about it and George's physical nature is undermined by Lettie because he lacks complete confidence in it.

The White Peacock is a slight book and is passed over by many commentators on Lawrence. Leavis dismisses it with the quotation from Lawrence, 'I was very young when I wrote the *Peacock* – I began it at twenty. Let that be my apology.'[13]

But what is perhaps more surprising is the way in which it contains – albeit in undeveloped form – the major preoccupations of his later books.

The opening chapter of *Sons and Lovers* depicts an essentially similar conflict to that just discussed in *The White Peacock*. This is not to deny that there are differences between Lettie Beardsall and George Saxton on the one hand and Gertrude Coppard and Walter Morel on the other and differences which in a different context and in the light of a different purpose would need to be carefully noted. But since the perspective I have taken is that of the essential characteristics of human nature as defined in *Studies in Classical American Literature* – in so far as it is possible to speak at all about such characteristics – my central task will be to note the similarities and any modifications which the new treatment might imply for the nature of the self.

Gertrude Coppard is a more clearly defined character than Lettie and so we can understand better the sources of her actions and therefore the structure of the self they reveal. She is not a culture-Philistine to the same degree as Lettie, though neither is she without pretensions. But the chief source of her dualism is religious. She is a puritan; the daughter of a parson, 'who drew near in sympathy only to one man, the Apostle Paul'.[14] The true self, for her, is identified with the spiritual or intellectual principle: 'She loved ideas and was considered very intellectual. What she liked most of all was an argument on religion or philosophy or politics with some educated man.'[15] But her dualism reflects its puritan origins and is heavier, more moralistic and lacks some of the flippancy of Lettie's. As Lettie despised George so Gertrude despises Morel and the gross unspiritual life he represents: 'His nature was purely sensuous and she strove to make him moral, religious.'[16] And so life in the Morel household is dominated by the conflict between the spiritual idealism of Gertrude and what she sees as the brutality of the life which her husband embodies. Lawrence himself is yet to gain a clear perspective on the weakness of his mother's idealism and the corresponding strength of the other side of life which she denied. And he was later to regret the portrayal of his father in this book, feeling that he had done him a great injustice. But whatever opinion Lawrence may have held of his father at this time and however he may have wanted to present him through the eyes of his mother, the novel again does not quite let him away with it. Gertrude and later Paul frequently express contempt for Morel and the brutal uncultured life he represents. But the book does not always permit the reader to identify with them. One reason for this lies in the fact that they never advert – as the book does – to the social conditions of which Morel is partly a product. It is true that like George Saxton he represents a physical life which Gertrude and Lettie find inimical to their own spiritual aspirations but more than this Morel represents that life brutalized by the physical conditions of his life and work. Therefore we detect a certain smugness in Paul's contempt for his father when he gets drunk on the way home from work or when he falls asleep at the table with his head resting on his arms, because the son shows no awareness of the degrading conditions which have brought him to this nor of the effects of the silent contempt in which he is held at home.

Again it is interesting to notice the change which occurs in Morel when the mode of his work is changed from the dehumanizing labour of the mines to work in whose result he can take pride:

> The only time when he entered again into the life of his own people
> was when he worked, and was happy at work. Sometimes, in the
> evenings, he cobbled the boots or mended the kettle or the pit-bottle.
> Then he always wanted several attendants, and the children enjoyed
> it. They united with him in the work, in the actual doing of something,
> when he was his real self again.[17]

For when his work is turned from *poesis* into *praxis* he shows glimpses of
that larger humanity which his work and his life have destroyed. In *Sons
and Lovers* Lawrence himself is scarcely conscious of this, let alone of
the social implications which lie behind it. But, again, the novel finds it
harder to lie than its author and whatever conscious designs he may have
upon us, the material is there which will enable us to make a better
judgement. The society represented by the culture and morality to which
Gertrude aspires, justifies its exclusion of what Morel represents; firstly
by placing it negatively – it is unspiritual and therefore physical and
coarse (as with Nietzsche's reflection on the word 'world', words which
begin as descriptive become terms of disparagement); then it imposes
upon him a brutalizing mode of life which alienates him from himself
and helps to construct for him a character which serves to justify the
original judgement. Like George Saxton, only more so, the standards
evoked and the life imposed ensure that Morel will have nothing of
which he can be proud.

Gertrude, then, will admit only the spiritual self; she is like
Dimmesdale in *The Scarlet Letter*. Significantly, in introducing
Dimmesdale and Hester in *Studies* Lawrence is reminded of the conflict
between his mother and father:

> My father hated books, hated the sight of anyone reading or
> writing.
> My mother hated the thought that any one of her sons should be
> condemned to manual labour. Her sons must have something higher
> than that.[18]

But Gertrude is not only the spiritual self she has chosen and hence the
conflict here too is interiorized. For, as *Studies* has insisted, we are not
the great choosers we think we are; society may try to impose, or like
Ligeia we ourselves may try to impose a certain concept of self but there
remains in us a basic residual nature which must be taken account of.

And so Gertrude will not be shut up within the puritan self she has chosen. This darker side of her nature makes itself felt in her attraction to Walter Morel, which has obviously nothing to do with her love of 'arguments in religion and philosophy'. In the dualistic language of *Studies* the conflict between the blood-consciousness and the mind-consciousness is already taking place in her. It is what the puritan in her represses that attracts her to Morel and she hates him because he has disturbed the slumber of that part of her self with which her chosen identity cannot cope. The very attempt at repression makes the demands of her physical nature more imperious:

> She was a puritan, like her father, high-minded and really stern. Therefore the dusky, golden softness of this man's sensuous flame of life, that flowed off his flesh like the flame from a candle, not baffled and gripped into incandescence by thought and spirit as her life was, seemed to her something wonderful, beyond her.[19]

And this is why sex is so important for Lawrence. It is almost as though without it the self could get away with its spiritual posing. The sexual experience forces towards the surface of consciousness dimensions of the self which lie outside the limits of its chosen identity. And with this attraction to Morel she even has a brief, startled fascination for the life of the miners:

> She looked at him, startled. This was a new tract of life suddenly opened before her. She realized the life of the miners, hundreds of them toiling below earth and coming up at evening. He seemed to her noble.[20]

But even here we see the essential unity of human consciousness asserting itself against its disintegration into blood and mind. When Gertrude sees the life of the miners as 'noble', her 'mental consciousness' is already interpreting in categories it can understand and accept, experiences which are essentially alien to it. But Gertrude never fully understands the nature of the conflict in her own soul and so can never achieve integrity. She is attracted to the dark world which Morel represents; for something in her self is a part of it. But the mental consciousness or the cultured self with which she identifies will not accept the other for what it is and so like Dimmesdale she sins against the only self she is prepared to recognize.

The same essential pattern of conflict is repeated when, having rejected Morel, she chooses to ground herself on her son William. Motherhood, with the desire to lift her son out of the mining community into 'something higher', becomes her new chosen identity. This choice bears in at least three ways on the problem of the self.

Firstly, the physical side of her nature which she has rejected with Morel, can find some unacknowledged satisfaction in an Oedipal relationship with her son and since this is unconscious it need not intrude upon her chosen identity. Furthermore, since this satisfaction is heavily disguised beneath the mother image, which, at least before Freud, was considered utterly spiritual, it is wholly within the aspirations of her puritan culture. And thirdly, because the ideal of motherhood within the Christian culture is allied to the idea of self-sacrifice and self-effacement, it can serve as a useful manoeuvre to divert attention from the development of that self with which her puritan morality is unable to cope. It is that same escape from the responsibility for the development of the self which Lawrence noted towards the end of *The White Peacock*.

While this compromise may temporarily solve some of the mother's problems, its effect upon the children is disastrous. William is the first to suffer. She refuses to allow him to become himself because both physically and spiritually she will not let him go. And so she is physically jealous of any girl of whom he becomes fond but, as well as this, she sees in his attraction to girls and dancing the emergence of the old physical nature she despises in Morel. She wants to see nothing in William which is not part of her chosen identity for him just as she denied anything in her own nature which conflicted with her chosen self. It is a repetition of the sin against the Holy Ghost.

And the Holy Ghost is within us. It is the thing that prompts us to be real, . . . not to be too egoistic and wilful in our conscious self, but to change as the spirit inside us bids us change.[21]

Gertrude's instinct now is to distrust this spirit; for it was at its bidding that she married Morel and in his coarse, passionate life she sees its work.

At the centre of the novel is Paul's quest for an identity, which displays many of the characteristics already noted and the same basic structure of the self outlined in *Studies*. Miriam Leivers is another spiritual soul; she chooses an ideal self whose origins are partly Christian and partly Romantic. But, whatever the origins, the effect of both is, as Nietzsche has shown, the same: each aims at the creation of a substitute reality which renders the world we live in coarse and unrefined. Hence she is sensitive, finding the physical side of life somewhat distasteful – 'The slightest grossness made her recoil almost in anguish' and: 'It could never be mentioned that the mare was in foal.'[22] Thus she leaves a whole area of her experience ignored and rejected in order to live her ideal of a spiritual existence and in contact with Paul she seeks a relationship which is entirely Platonic. This is the self she has chosen but, as *Studies* was to maintain, the other self of the dark forest is always there to threaten it:

> . . . there was a serpent in her Eden. She searched earnestly in herself to see if she wanted Paul Morel. She felt there would be some disgrace in it. Full of twisted feeling, she was afraid she did want him. She stood self-convicted. Then came an agony of new shame. She shrank within herself in a coil of torture.[23]

She finds in herself that grossness which makes her recoil when she meets it in the outside world or in the conversation of others and her integrity begins to split. But then the mental consciousness starts its work, trying to construct a new integrity on its own terms. Recognizing the threat to her spiritual identity she begins to pray: she asks God to prevent her loving Paul. But in giving the name 'love' to this unhallowed feeling for Paul she transforms it and saves herself. 'Love was God's gift.' Eros has become Agape; and she reflects, perhaps it is God's wish that, in love, she should sacrifice herself to Paul.

It is a fiendish solution. Abraham and Isaac. Miriam, realizing that sexual love threatens to destroy her spiritual self, attempts to transcend the loss by shifting ground and making it a part of a new spiritual ideal of self-sacrifice. For Lawrence, the sex experience is the most potent solution for dissolving the structures of mental consciousness but Miriam will insulate herself from its effects by calling sexual love self-sacrifice and attempting to experience it as such. As a result the description of their sexual encounter in terms of religious sacrifice is truly ghastly.

Thus the ideal consciousness continues to assert itself; Miriam will not relax, will not leave herself to 'the great hunger and impersonality of passion'. Paul, weary now of the effort to sustain his spiritual identity, feeling that a part of his nature is being starved, seeks relief in the *impersonality* of passion but Miriam will not let go: 'He could not bear it. "Leave me alone – leave me alone," he wanted to cry; but she wanted him to look at her with eyes full of love.'[24] She wants the experience sterilized and transformed into one which her ideal self can accept so that she can go through it with her chosen personality intact. But Paul wants none of this: 'He seemed to be almost unaware of her as a person: she was only to him then a woman. She was afraid'.[25] The personality which she seeks to maintain, Paul strives to destroy; for, to him, it is nothing but a construct of the will: 'To be rid of our individuality, which is our will, which is our effort – to live effortless, a kind of conscious sleep – that is very beautiful, I think; that is our after-life – our immortality.'[26] The idea of personality as that which has to be destroyed as a prelude to authentic existence is undeveloped here. We should like to say looking back from the theoretical standpoint of *Studies* that the personality being eroded is to be identified with the mental-consciousness and it is destroyed so that the blood-consciousness, with the enlarged experience which it entails, might regenerate the lives of Paul and Miriam. And indeed in Miriam we can see an early exemplification of the heavy mental consciousness which Lawrence exposes in the wilful Ligeia and a mode of life which he is later to identify – as I think wrongly – with Nietzsche's notion of 'will to power'. But the relationship between Miriam and Paul leads to no such enlargement. Furthermore, should we be led to attribute this to Miriam's spirituality, we will find that he encounters the same failure with Clara Dawes. He remains his mother's creature with no coherent alternative to the personality he seeks to destroy. In rejecting the only personality of which he can conceive, he seeks his own annihilation and so as he leaves Miriam he wonders, 'Why did the thought of death and the after-life seem so consoling?'

Paul seeks the obliteration of his personality in passion and there is in his attitude the Romantic alliance between sex and death; a fascination with corruption which seeks release from the real world. It produces the same resentment against reality as the dualism of either Gertrude or Miriam. For Paul, on the one hand, wants to affirm the supreme importance of the body – thus insisting on a dimension of reality and life which Miriam denies – but at the same time he is seeking through the dissolution of his personality in sexual experience an escape from reality. The pose which he adopts at the end of the book, walking towards the city with clenched fists, resembles all too closely the attitude of the nineteenth-century Romantic pessimist, which Nietzsche diagnosed as the central weakness in the otherwise much-admired Schopenhauer. For Schopenhauer, he thought, had surpassed all his contemporaries by seeing the world, not as the project of some divine intelligence, nor as the man-made and man-centred Utopia of David Strauss and the socialists, but as it is – 'an episode unprofitably disturbing the blessed calm of nothingness'.[27]

But for Nietzsche, Schopenhauer is here evoking standards to which his realism can lay no claim. For he only succeeds in slandering this life by painting the nothing, which this life has disturbed, in pleasing and seductive colours and in so doing draws liberally on his readings in Eastern philosophy. And when Paul Morel seeks the annihilation of his personality, individuality and will and the cessation of all effort the sentiment and the language itself is Schopenhauer's.[28] Furthermore the attraction which this process of dissolution exercises on Paul and on the reader depends largely on Lawrence's capacity to present the process in the same lurid imagery as Schopenhauer.

But what are the real origins of this pessimism? Paul's failure and that of many other characters in the book derives largely from their lack of realism, from their continued attempts to have life on *their* terms and their subsequent disillusionment when reality kicks back and refuses to be confined within their limited concepts of it. Each has a vision of the world as it might be, purged of all grossness beside which reality, then, appears as a poor imitation. For Nietzsche there is one solution to all these difficulties: throw the myths over, break the idols and look at the world as it is, innocent now because there is no ideal now which it can be accused of failing to reach. And much of Lawrence's own work succeeds in injecting a good dose of realism into the ideal conception of man. But will reality become wholly acceptable, as Nietzsche suggests, when we cease to falsify it? Are all negative life-denying attitudes traceable to such dualisms?

Paul's experience of his mother's death adds to his pessimism. In spite of the confusion which philosophers and others have spread about this subject since the beginning of the nineteenth century, there are two attitudes to death which can be distinguished. Either the individual human personality survives the death of the body and death is the beginning of some new experience, or it does not and death is the end of all experience. If we believe in personal immortality, and as is usual, conceive of our new life as inestimably superior to this life, then the idea of death can become the ground upon which we are alienated from the world. This is Nietzsche's complaint and, of course, it has been a common characteristic of some Christian practice, though it should be noticed that other Christian theologians have seen belief in personal immortality not as focusing attention on an alternative existence against which this one is devalued, but as giving depth and intelligibility to an existence which would otherwise be absurd. Nevertheless this belief has been and can always become a source of alienation. If, on the other hand, we believe in death as total annihilation what consequent view should we take of life? Some philosophers, like Nietzsche, will maintain that once the delusion of an afterlife is shattered man will be more easily reconciled to this one; its very transience will make it lighter and sweeter. The thought of death will produce that 'precious and fragrant drop of levity' which will invigorate the whole of life. So that for Nietzsche that pessimism which feeds on death is no different from that which draws on romantic myths or spiritual delusions; and the cure is the same: abandon the myths, in this case the delusion of personal immortality, and the thought of death will cease to poison the whole of life. But confronted with our actual experience of death – as Paul is in *Sons and Lovers* – Nietzsche's solution appears facile. The desire for permanence in human relationships and in being will not be lightly cast off and Camus testifies that when all man's myths have been exploded, his experience of death remains irreducible and renders the world upon which it is based wholly unacceptable. For him the only response is the rebel's, who in resisting death affirms the supreme value of life. But he remains unreconciled with the world and his rebellion always ends in defeat.

The evidence which would enable us to decide this question finally is not available. However we do not observe in the failure of the recurrent attempts by Stoic philosophers like Marcus Aurelius to convince themselves that death is natural and nothing to be feared nor in the experience of twentieth-century societies where belief in personal immortality is moribund, any diminution in the revulsion of people against the prospect of death. There are those, it is true, like Herbert Marcuse, who foresee the eventual triumph over all fear of death. Marcuse's optimism is the prophet's rather than the scientist's and as it stands placed against our brute experience of death it is a hope and must take its place beside those other hopes by which man has tried to reconcile himself to the reality of death. To Nietzsche it would be nothing but an alternative delusion to belief in personal immortality.

The attitude of Schopenhauer is confusing on this point. For he wishes to maintain both that death is annihilation and, at the same time, that the resultant state of non-being is something to be desired. So that death without immortality still retains the capacity for alienation which the concept of personal immortality possessed. Paul Morel too will describe death with all the language of negation and yet will use it as a ground upon which to slander life. After his failure with Miriam:

To him now, life seemed a shadow, day a white shadow; night, and death, and stillness, and inaction, this seemed like *being*. To be alive, to be urgent and insistent – that was *not-to-be*. The highest of all was to melt out into the darkness and sway there identified with the great Being.[29]

And when his mother dies, darkness and death are invested with richer qualities still:

> Everywhere the vastness and terror of the immense night which is roused and stirred for a brief while by the day, but which returns, and will remain at last eternal, holding everything in its silence and its living gloom. There was no Time, only Space. Who could say his mother had lived and did not live? She had been in one place, and was in another; that was all. And his soul could not leave her wherever she was. Now she was gone abroad into the night, and he was with her still. They were together.[30]

She had been in one place, and was in another. Does this suggest a belief in personal immortality? We cannot say because the attitude of the book is ambivalent and the passages on death expressed in the language of nineteenth-century German Idealism with all the confusion which this allows. It evokes perfectly the inner confusion of Paul himself; death is seen at once as the bed-rock of reality, the place where he and his mother are together, but at the same time it is the place of 'vastness and terror' where everything is held in 'silence' and 'living gloom'. It both attracts and repels and causes the fluctuations between life and death which are characteristic of Paul in the second half of the book. And in spite of his rejection of the dark in the end and his stoical walk towards 'the faintly glowing humming town', the impression remains of him as of someone still ill-equipped for life and with a strong holding in death.

But there is more. For Lawrence begins to see in the resistance against death a certain irreverence. Paul is horrified at his mother's will to live: 'If I had to die, I'd will to die.'[31] The particular will must submerge itself in the universal will. There is something of Ligeia here, the expression in Gertrude of the same will which sought to determine its own nature at the outset of her adult life. Nature resisted her then as it does now in a more peremptory way. For in death nature finally reveals that the self is not merely the construct of the will, that we are not the great choosers we think. Human nature is revealed finally as derivative and contingent. Death and sex, therefore, have this in common: they undermine our pretensions to be the sole creators of the self. Man has not become God.

These two books then present us with many *cul-de-sacs* on the way to the realization of the self. These are diverse but all possess in some degree the element detected in *Studies* and described variously as dualism, idealism and the dominance of the will. They consist in some attempt to distort reality by conceiving it according to some dead conceptual pattern. Whether it is a Christian spirituality which hates the world because it is not heaven or the body because it kills the soul; or a romantic spirituality which schools itself to see the world as it never was and is made uneasy by occasional glimpses of reality; they are both expressions of what Nietzsche called resentment – resentment against life. The novels have shown this by the continual confrontation between characters in some way or other affected by ideas and the life which those ideas make possible.

It is like the process which Lawrence envisaged in his criticism of the Platonic dialogue where he suggested the interruption of the philosophic argument by some dramatic incident. But whereas the purpose of the dialogue was to examine the relation between different concepts and to test for inconsistencies – a process which the little furore suggested by Lawrence would only hinder – the purpose of the novel is different; for it wishes to submit these ideas to a different kind of test, the test of lived experience as recreated in the novel.

How do these ideas, consistent or inconsistent by philosophical standards, function when the protagonist who possesses them or who is possessed by them, is placed by his creator in a chosen stretch of life? It is this test that so many characters in the novel fail but in their different though related failures a picture of those dimensions of life which they destroy begins to emerge. It is never, and never can be, encapsulated within a new set of concepts, but by a kind of *via negativa* some of its contours are indicated.

4 The Self and Society: *The Rainbow*

In Sons and Lovers society, when it begins to structure and determine the nature of the self, is almost always seen as destructive of those possibilities for life which a self liberated from it might attain. But in Paul's painting there is an exception; for through it society presents him with a mode of personal growth. It is the one instance in the novel where something which derives from society and culture also offers uncontaminated opportunities for such growth. However some hesitation is caused by the fact that the position which Paul's painting occupies in the transmission and development of that social mode to which it belongs is never clearly shown. We are never made aware of the community to which Paul as painter belongs nor of the precise nature of his problems in painting and their possible bearing on the problem of life. We might put it differently by saying that, while we are told often enough that Paul's concern with painting is serious, we are never shown anything which would lead us to suspect that the problems to which he addresses himself as an artist are any more significant than those of a mere dabbler. The reason for this is undoubtedly that Lawrence says painting when he means writing and that, therefore, the precise nature of the aesthetic mode to which he refers and its particular bearing on life cannot be clearly indicated. On balance then, when we set the creative potential of Paul's painting against the destructive force of the social aspirations of Gertrude and Miriam, the self seems more disabled than strengthened by those elements of social life which are allowed to become constitutive of it.

But in the opening of *The Rainbow* this emphasis is changed. In the outward-looking aspirations of the women of the Marsh, who want something other than blood intimacy, education and the wider social world are seen as giving power, dominance, freedom and extended being. By comparison there is something dead, regressive and even hostile to life in the desire of the men to remain static, to resist change and to accept a self based solely on the old blood intimacy.[1]

No longer are the aspirations of the women for education and culture seen only as burdens from the past which pervert the developing life of men. They are not seen here as they were in Lettie, Gertrude and Miriam as sources of impotence and resentment but as positive projections into the future. And so we can say of a life exclusively given over to blood intimacy what Lawrence was to say later in *Studies* of Melville's life with the South Sea Islanders:

> We can't go back . . . we cannot turn the current of our life backwards . . . . We can only do it when we are renegade. The renegade hates life itself. He wants the death of life. So these many 'reformers' and 'idealists' who glorify the savages in America. They are death-birds, life-haters. Renegades.
>
> We can't go back. And Melville couldn't. Much as he hated the civilized humanity he knew.[2]

Seen against this insight, what the women of the Marsh have to offer is something constructive and vital. For the mythology of the simple natural life is as much a delusion as any of the ideal conceptions urged by the women of the earlier novels.

However, the women are unclear about the exact contours of the extended being to which they aspire; it is sensed rather than apprehended and consequently their attempts to direct their sons towards it are not always efficacious. They vaguely identify the power of this extended being with the vicar, as did Gertrude in *Sons and Lovers*. There is therefore about them a certain aura of the old spirituality which is destructive and so they frequently impose upon their sons modes of being which are as sterile as the masculine alternative. Thus Tom Brangwen begins life deriving from the womenfolk the same disabling dualism as Paul Morel. From his home at the Marsh he gets the idea of woman as the symbol for a larger life which comprises religion, love and morality. This creates in him a desire to find in woman the embodiment of his own inarticulate religious impulses. But at the same time he is tormented with sex desires and his imagination reverts always to lustful scenes.[3] He never finds satisfaction; for his relationships with women always reveal themselves in what they lack. They are unable to bear the burden of the expectations he puts upon them.

But the positive dimensions of the women's aspirations evoked in the opening pages are not lost and Tom catches some of them. He is not, therefore, without some sensitivity to the world beyond the Marsh and hence the fascination exercised on him by the foreign gentleman and the woman at Matlock. He is attracted by this man's tact, by his reserve, by his gracious manner, indeed by everything about him which conjures up possibilities of a life so different from that which Tom knows. Though the man is in many ways attractive – he has 'a cold animal intelligence . . . a monkey-like self surety' – to Tom he represents all those uncharted areas of experience towards which the women of the Marsh have directed him and in the end the couple 'set fire to the homestead of his nature'.[4] His old self is being destroyed as he is given the sense of enlarged possibilities. But he is attracted to the couple in more ways than one. For in his imagination he does not separate his feeling for what the man represents from the feeling of physical satisfaction he has in the presence of the woman. And so for the first time, in a curiously gratuitous way, his disparate feelings for woman are welded together. He is able to indulge his sense of physical satisfaction without forsaking that larger responsibility upon which the women of the Marsh had insisted.

But the union is unsatisfactory. Firstly, because there is no organic connection between his sense of physical satisfaction in the woman and the sense of enlarged life represented by her companion. Although the two experiences are vaguely united in Tom's imagination, they remain in reality quite distinct. As yet he can see no way of conceiving the two as part of a single organic pursuit. And secondly, his sense of the larger world represented by the foreigner is vague and imperfectly conceived so that it cannot play a decisive part in his development. The self has been prised open to accept experiences whose form and significance can never really become a part of it until they are more fully understood.

In the meeting with Lydia Lensky the first of these difficulties is overcome. The foreigner and the woman are now one and in Tom's courtship of her his dualistic sensibilities are welded together till they become almost indistinguishable. The mystery of sex, that dimension of human experience which belongs to the blood-consciousness and which *Studies* placed beyond any possible conceptualization, is heightened by the mystery of the foreigner in Lydia, which is also inaccessible to any conceptualization of which Tom is capable. From both sources, therefore, the relationship is prohibited from creating any finished self much as the relationship between Chingachgook and Natty Bumppo excluded the pocket-sized self of Benjamin Franklin. It is a relationship which develops apart from and in spite of the spoken word. The difference in language and the difference in culture which this implies rarely allow either to comprehend what the other says.

When she talked of Poland or of what had been, it was all so foreign, she scarcely communicated anything to him. And when he looked at her, an over-much reverence and fear of the unknown changed the nature of his desire into a sort of worship, holding her aloof from his physical desire, self-thwarting.[5]

This is both the relationship's strength and its weakness; its strength because it keeps it free from any conceptualization that might distort it. Lydia remains so essentially incomprehensible to Tom that he is never tempted to seek that kind of conceptual knowledge which Lawrence exposed as so destructive in his essay on Poe. Tom has a reverence, even 'an over-much reverence' for her which protects him completely from that kind of spiritual arrogance.

But, on the other hand, he frequently fails to understand and to respond to what Lydia feels and desires. After his proposal to her, she is for the first time open and receptive to another person; she is 'attentive and instinctively expectant before him'. The whole experience has all the possibilities of a rebirth for her. But Tom understands none of this and once he has her acceptance he withdraws and forces the relationship into the mould of a 'proper' English courtship.[6] This is not simply a matter of chastity; it is the intrusion of a publicly sanctioned form of behaviour in a relationship where it manifestly has no place. And it is paradoxically a situation where more, not less, knowledge is required to protect the two individuals from a clumsy and inappropriate sense of themselves and their significance for each other. For the introjection of social norms is not always a conscious process.

And so Lydia closes up again and is quite oblivious of Tom and then it is his turn to fret and rage so that in the end he fails to take hold of those possibilities from the larger world which Lydia represents. His conception of them remains unformed and finally relapses into the old blood-intimacy of life at the Marsh. He never comes to possess any of those characteristics which his perception of the wider world evoked and he remains, in spite of his occasional successes with Lydia, essentially unfulfilled.

She is really too foreign for him. A foreign presence can extend the self to embrace the new possibilities which it offers but if that presence is utterly foreign, if the self can find no foothold in it at all, it will be thrown back and any contact between the two becomes merely 'sensational'. It is another instance of 'a something about which nothing can be said' and Lydia comes to feel the negation of herself in Tom's approaches to her. She wants him to know, she says, that there is something there besides himself. But he comes to her as though for nothing, as though she were nothing, as though there were nothing there.[7] The mystery of the other person is one thing and, as Lawrence sees, an essential element in the extension of the self, but there is a limit to the distance which may exist between the two if effective growth is to be possible.

In the end he comes to accept her at the level of passion as something wholly other. He seeks in her 'the blazing kernel of darkness' and his own destruction.[8] It is the old blood-intimacy of the Marsh and Lydia's foreign-ness functions now only in that direction; it no longer suggests to him anything from the wider social world and in the end he gives up all such aspirations. His last flirtation with them occurs when, in his desire to make Anna a lady, he goes to visit his brother's mistress. She is an educated lady who reads Browning and Herbert Spencer.

In her presence he feels like a prisoner cut off from all those forms of life which lie outside of him. It is the same feeling evoked by the foreigner at Matlock but weaker now after his experience of marriage to Lydia and in the end he goes away feeling that there is something cold and alien about her — 'an inhuman being who used up human life for cold, unliving purposes'.[9] The idea of culture here has reverted to the negative sense of the earlier novels.

And so, when these ideas are abandoned, Tom goes back to seek an older integrity in which he accepts his passionate fulfilment with Lydia as well as his long periods of frustration. He accepts Lydia, with all her incomprehensibility just as, in his capacity as farmer, he accepts the changes in the weather and the seasons without understanding the purpose which lies behind them. For he sees himself as part of a larger whole whose designs are utterly incomprehensible to him. Hence his experiences on those long February nights when the ewes are in labour and he sits looking at the stars and feels himself small and submissive to some greater purpose.[10] He continues to see his own life and that of Lydia as a part of this greater order and therefore there is much about it he is prepared to accept however unsatisfactory it may seem to him. Human purposes — willed purposes, we might say — are nothing within the eternal motions of nature of which they are a part. During Lydia's labour he reflects, 'There was the infinite world, eternal, unchanging, as well as the world of life.'[11] Tom certainly finds some satisfaction in these speculations but they ultimately erode that responsibility for the development of the self upon which Lawrence lays such great stress.

Studies outlined three possible views of the nature of the self: 1. It is a product of nature; 2. It is the product of man's will and the social structures he creates; 3. It is partly determined by nature and partly by human choice. Tom Brangwen comes to take the first of these views and commits himself to that form of personal and social irresponsibility which fails to distinguish between those aspects of the self which are given in nature and those which are the responsibility of the individual's action both on his own personal life and on those social and political structures of which he is a part. There is always a danger in attempting to subsume concepts of personal and social life under concepts of nature. As we have seen, Aristotle is the great offender here and nothing so clearly illustrates the danger as his disgraceful conclusion that slavery was a natural institution. It is precisely in seeing such things as natural that men lose the capacity to change them. Tom can progress no further in one direction with Lydia because he accepts as 'natural', and therefore as inevitable, a relationship in which there are long periods of frustration and virtually no communication, at least at the level of thought and language.

The relationship between Tom and Lydia finally becomes one of blood-intimacy, a relationship downwards where the dark self is secure from the intrusion of language and concept. But the self thus secured encapsulates nothing of the outward social aspirations of the women of the Marsh. This produces both the security and its attendant isolation which is seen in the family life of the Brangwens.

The little family is separated from the world and it achieves poise and independence. To Tom and Lydia the outside world becomes a matter of indifference, while to the young Anna it is a hostile presence. Lydia's horizon is 'staked out and marked' by her immediate family – 'a law to themselves, separate from the world, isolated, a small republic set in invisible bounds'.[12] Tom has grounded himself entirely in this intimacy and in so far as he belongs wholly to nature he is secure. But in another direction he is diminished; he is completely indifferent to the common values of the world. And he *is* reduced because he has abandoned his original aspirations to a larger self. Furthermore, the conceptual distinction here should not mislead us into thinking that it represents two real possibilities. There is no question of Tom Brangwen, or anyone else, having an option between a natural and a social self. For the choosing individual is already implicated in both worlds and in part defined by them. A human self can never simply be a product of nature, however much we may wish it so, nor can it grow to its horizons in 'a deep inarticulate interchange'. Language is not merely the characteristic of the inauthentic self deriving from society; not merely the mould in which the dummy standards of society are fixed. It is a characteristic with which *any* self, individual or social, is constituted.

And so the family life itself is threatened by this taste for the inarticulate. Anna feels the need for greater intelligibility but when she comes to Brangwen with her uncertainties he becomes uneasy because he does 'not want to have things dragged into consciousness'.[13] And more often than not, this means not facing them at all.

It is useful at this point to note briefly the place which language holds in the development of the self. It is an ambivalent one. For, on the one hand, language is essentially a public and a social thing and so carries all the dangers to personal authenticity which this implies. On the other hand, in speaking about the self at all we are talking about something which uses a language, and not accidentally either, but which is to a large extent defined in that very activity. Lawrence frequently speaks about the growth and development of the self but such expressions can have no intelligibility apart from some idea of an increasing sophistication in discriminating experience through the use of concepts. For experience and knowledge are always dependent on the acquisition of the relevant concepts. And again is not language the chosen medium of the author of *The Rainbow*? Wittgenstein once commented that 'Philosophy is a battle against the bewitchment of our intelligence by means of language'.[14] But he knew also that this battle was carried on in language. This serves to underline the point noticed in *Studies* that the self is in part a social phenomenon. Those characters, like Tom Brangwen, in whom the drive towards the inarticulate becomes extreme, are in effect denying themselves the possibility of development in this direction.

In fact this is what happens to Tom. In turning away from the spoken word he is also turning away from that world to which it belongs. Anna cannot survive within these horizons because, like her father before her, she experiences the need to grow in a way which is not possible inside this 'small republic set in invisible bounds'.[15]

The Marsh to her is like the torture cell of a certain French bishop in which the victim could neither stand up nor lie down. In Will she sees the possibility of escape. She is initially attracted by his talk about architecture; the very words thrill her, opening as they do on a wider world of culture and the possibility of a more articulate self. To her he is 'the hole in the wall beyond which the sunshine blazed on an outside world'.[16] And from then on she begins 'to act independently of her parents and to live beyond them'.[17]

In this Tom is made aware of his own failure and of the limitations of his chosen life. He is placed finally in the past. The aspirations he had for another world and the possibilities for the self which they implied are revealed now as lost and he himself is 'a man put apart with those whose life has no more developments'.[18] Looking on his own life he finds that, in spite of all his satisfactions, something is missing. What had his life been, he asks, but a 'long marital embrace with his wife'?[19] In the end he retains a bitterness that he must remain unsatisfied. That 'further, creative life', which he had missed, is now with Anna.

Will Brangwen appears as a person living at a different level and in some respects at a higher level than Tom. To Anna he is a representative of culture and society. By establishing a relationship with him, she hopes to extend herself beyond the stifling intimacy of the Marsh. However in Will the novel takes a new look at the self enlarged, or apparently enlarged, to those extremities envisaged by the young Tom Brangwen under the influence of the women of the Marsh. For in spite of the promise which he embodies for Anna, she destroys him and with him those dimensions of the self which he represents. The process of his disintegration is presented by Lawrence with scrupulous care but I shall trace only its very general contours as they can be contained in the concepts already discussed in *Studies in Classic American Literature*. In this we shall see that Will is a paradigm of that self which is forced to betray those beliefs in which it was grounded and that this betrayal is accelerated by the static way in which those beliefs are apprehended and by Will's failure to give them their relevant articulation. At the end of this section Lawrence identifies Will's collapse with his failure to become sufficiently articulate.

This is important. For Lawrence frequently inveighs against the influence of conceptual knowledge on the self; it nails it down, inhibiting any new development. Nevertheless a part of Will's failure is traced to his inability to gain a sufficiently clear perspective on his aspirations and their implications, which suggests, as Birkin says later, that it is not concepts as such which destroy the growing self but its imprisonment within a false set of concepts. The deeper sense of life which he has from religion, for example, is destroyed when he reflects upon the literal meaning of the words in which it is expressed but this is only because those words have been removed from 'the stream of life' which alone gives them meaning. And, of course, the deeper social reason is the disintegration of the form of life itself.

The first shock comes for Will when in the early weeks of their marriage Anna and he shut themselves off 'in tacit denial of the world'.[20] He feels guilty at not behaving like 'a decent social being'.[21] But the experience changes the centre of his being and he can no longer return to his old social self with any conviction because by contrast with his new life with Anna it has lost much of its reality for him. Part of the reason for this is that Will's hold upon the other life is insecure anyway and

Anna later exploits this by persistently questioning him about his carving, the Church, etc. The inadequacy of the relationship is partly due to Anna and partly to Will. For Anna, in spite of her early dissatisfaction with the close intimacy of life at the Marsh and her apparent craving for the open road which characterized the earlier part of her relationship with Will, is in the end unwilling to risk herself to the unknown either in her own nature or beyond it. She is disturbed when she finds that Will is more than just a 'bright reflex of herself', that he does not alter and remains 'a dark opposite to her'.[22] It is not that there is nothing in her that can respond to the mysterious extension of being which he offers but rather that she is afraid, 'ashamed', she says, of those desires which take her beyond her known self. 'She wanted to be like other people, *decently* satisfied.'[23] She has not the courage for what *Studies* described as 'the bravest doctrine man had ever proposed to himself'. In the end she wants to be bound up, confined within the limits of what she can know. She worships human knowledge and, we are told, believes in 'the omnipotence of the human mind'.[24] In spite of all her aspirations, the self she chooses is the self she can know. She is consumed with a wild passion for the unknown. But she is in dread of it and so she clings tenaciously to her known self.[25] She finishes unsatisfied and like the other women of the Marsh looks into the distance with a sense that there is something beyond her in which she has not taken part. She feels a certain sense of guilt in having failed to play her full part and having abandoned responsibility for her personal development. But then like so many of the women in Lawrence's novels she takes refuge in the old pretext that child-bearing is her part and that perhaps the children will have the courage which she lacked. And so she relinquishes her adventure to the unknown with the excuse that she is bearing her children. Then she lapses back into a vague content, and the self which in the beginning she had struggled to create remains inchoate.

Will Brangwen is a complex character. Through his love of painting, architecture and the Church he is a part of a wide tradition and culture which provides a framework within which his passionate nature can develop. For he belongs, as *Studies* expressed it, 'to a living, organic, *believing* community, active in fulfilling some unfulfilled, perhaps unrealized purpose'. But on the other hand his understanding of that tradition is imperfect and his horizons are set by what he can understand. The passionate side of his nature Anna fears and the other she ridicules. But while the two can be conceptually distinguished, in reality they combine to produce a single though complex character so that when Anna ridicules his attempts to articulate his feelings she is also jeering at his soul.

> The deep root of his enmity lay in the fact that she jeered at his soul. He was inarticulate and stupid in thought. But to some things he clung passionately.[26]

And what the novel goes on to show – perhaps beyond the author's conscious intention – is that the soul cannot really be distinguished from its 'thought'. It may be more than its thought but the thinking processes, in their breadth and their limitations, are in part constitutive of the self and its experience of the world.

This is nowhere more clearly illustrated than in the argument which he and Anna have about the Marriage Feast at Cana. Will's deep nature finds the story compelling, an essential part of his emotional life. Then Anna attacks it at the level of fact: How can he believe that ordinary rain water could become grape-juice? Intellectually he is compelled to accept her criticisms and to reject the story as a description of an historical event. But in doing so he is guilty of a 'violation of himself' because what he now knows to be factually false remains 'true for him'. The dilemma is one which delighted Kierkegaard who defined truth precisely in relation to such situations. 'Truth', he says, 'is an objective uncertainty held fast in an appropriation process of the most passionate inwardness.'[27] And he goes on to claim that the more objectively uncertain a proposition the more passionate intensity its acceptance will involve. If, he argues, something is certain then no passion will be involved in our adherence to it. Therefore the most compelling truths are those paradoxes which make up the core of Christian doctrine. At times, as when he sets up the opposition between the intellect and the blood-consciousness, Lawrence opts for a solution which is surprisingly similar. For both, passion becomes the criterion of truth. Their respective concepts of passion can only be distinguished when we view the kind of life to which they lead; Kierkegaard's is one of other-worldly asceticism and Lawrence's, while it can never be regarded as wholly free from the spiritual, is nevertheless more intimately bound up with the life of the body. *The Rainbow*, however, does not allow the simple dualism nor the 'suicide of reason' implicit in either solution. Will's failure to effect the integrity of passion and reason results in a failure to achieve an integrated self; it becomes, indeed, a violation of himself.

With Anna, then, Will is destroyed in those beliefs in which he had grounded himself and the process is continued in the chapter 'The Cathedral', in which yet 'another of his vital illusions' is destroyed. As a result his life shifts its centre and becomes more superficial. 'He had failed to become really articulate, failed to find real expression. He had to continue in the old form. But in spirit he was uncreated.'[28] Without the necessary articulation and expression the life forms of culture dry up and they become the prison of the spirit rather than the essential structures of its growth. His life, Lawrence comments, had been formed in 'unquestioned concepts' and concepts, when they are unquestioned, have ceased to grow and develop; they are static and complete and can never form an open structure within which the self can develop. Hence Will lapses back. He continues to serve the Church even more attentively now that he knows it to be false but he is no longer committed to it as a form of personal growth. He is aware of what he has lost and it is nothing less than the possibility of extended being; in the centre of himself there is something unformed which now will never ripen. And so he submits to the limitations of his being. Like Tom before him he is giving up the struggle and seeing himself as essentially limited. But in Will's resignation there is none of the old Nature mysticism by which Tom was enabled to attribute his failure to a larger, unintelligible purpose and in the expression 'limitation of his being' there is a greater degree of personal responsibility accepted. For it is not without the suggestion that he himself is partly the creator of that limited being and certainly it is not the product of some greater will whose purposes, if he could comprehend them, would be better than his own. The failure to achieve integrity is not surpassed in any higher synthesis and hence it remains nothing but a failure and the demand for something more like success becomes peremptory.

At home Will becomes submissive to Anna and really ceases to have any purpose of his own. She has overcome him and he acquiesces in her judgements. He cannot stand up to her and he cannot argue with her and though he knows she has destroyed something vital in him, he is still forced to submit to her. He becomes merely an adjunct of her will and inwardly he seethes with resentment. For that potency, whose outward and free expression she has made impossible, remains coiled up inside, poisoning him.

Then, in his encounter with the girl in Nottingham, it finds expression and he achieves a certain independence. For he is able to dominate her physically and he enjoys the sense of power which this gives him. His awareness of this power remains with him when he returns to Anna and he stands up to her physically in a way he never could intellectually and achieves a kind of independence, a kind of selfhood. And, we are told, this violent activity in his personal life sets another man in him free. He becomes firmly established in his public interests. He develops a real purposeful self.[29] But the force of the word 'real' depends upon the purpose towards which this new self is directed and its capacity to extend and develop. The interest he now takes in education is no substitute for those vital illusions which Anna destroyed. He has acquiesced in a dualism between his personal and public life which, while it frees him for a calmer participation in the public, limits his personal growth to what he can achieve in private. There is no integral connection between the two. So, having separated himself from Anna and having faced her as an equal in their physical life, he achieves a confidence in himself which spills over into his public life. But the self with which he is left has become fragmented and he is essentially unfulfilled.

Nor can his private encounters with Anna, with all the new assurance and sense of power he feels in them, be seen as unequivocally beneficial. For Will they are the expression of 'a lust for discovery' and in each he dwells upon one of 'the multitudinous beauties of her body'. Each day he spends brooding upon which one it is to be that night so that he is sent 'slightly insane'.[30] With the initial emphasis on the will to dominate, the insatiable quest for knowledge – even when it is called sensuous knowledge – the mechanical way in which different parts of the body are chosen night after night and finally the obsessive brooding which fills his days, we cannot but be reminded of Poe's Ligeia and Lawrence's justifiable castigation of her. The only outcome of the Ligeia relationship was final disintegration of the self and death. And of Will and Anna he comments, 'It was all lust and the infinite, maddening intoxication of the senses, a passion of death.'[31] The sense, therefore, in which the book can give meaning to the statement that through all this Will has achieved 'a real purposive self' is very limited indeed.

Thus he never achieves that authentic selfhood which Lawrence regards as normative. Firstly, because he never really abandons his belief that the old symbols of the Church and the culture of which they are a part are necessary to him. Then, because he fails to articulate this need adequately, he abandons any serious pursuit of such development. Next, his sexual life with Anna, excluding now the involvement of his total nature, declines into a purely physical encounter, expressing that desire for dominance which has been frustrated in the rest of their relationship. And finally, his life falls into a public/private dualism with little connection between the two.

From the start young Ursula Brangwen seeks a larger self than is possible in Cossethay. On going to Grammar School she is relieved to break out from the narrow life of Cossethay and from the limited people who live there.[32] Domestic life in the Brangwen house amid 'storms of babies' is inimical to such development. Reality in this form is too oppressive. She has that same outward vision which appeared in the earliest pages of the novel and if she is to grow she must find some point of reference outside of Cossethay.

She first seeks escape in Romantic literature, weaving herself an illusion from *Idylls of the Kings* which is rudely broken by her younger brothers and sisters and the insensitivity of her father. This illusion is an essential aid to her growth and can do little harm provided she does not hang on to it when it has exhausted its usefulness, as Miriam did in *Sons and Lovers*. What begins as 'a breath of inspiration' must not become in the end 'a fixed and evil form, which coils in round like mummy clothes'.[33]

The self, as we have seen, cannot be fixed in any predetermined pattern. For the young Ursula, however, her romantic illusion does not operate as a fixed idea but as a lever keeping open possibilities beyond the present. At this stage it does not much matter that the life envisaged is a rather vulgar romanticism; what is important for the young Ursula is that it focusses her attention on something better which she understands in concepts like 'spirituality', 'stateliness', etc. This 'intricately woven illusion of life' is quickly dropped and for it she substitutes the new illusion of school. She loves her Latin, Greek and French and she even experiences her algebraic equations as a great liberation.[34]

In this sense of freedom is expressed her release from all that pent-up frustration experienced by those generations of Brangwens to whom the clear articulation of the word was denied and who frequently raged under the burden of vague and half-understood feelings. For Ursula there is no contradiction between this delight in precise expression and her sense of the absolute, of the inexpressible, which she has from her father. And furthermore she sees from the start that there is no need always to insist upon the *literal* interpretation of the symbolic.

Ursula rejects her mother's immersion in the practical and opts instead for her father's thirst for the absolute. This gives her an interest in religion which shows itself particularly in her love for Sunday and for the place which the Church's year plays in her life. In the chapter 'The Widening Circle' Lawrence presents us with a different view of religion to that given in *Studies* or in the earlier novels.

Previously religion was seen largely as a form of other-worldly puritanism, alienating the self from its proper concerns. It prevented the development of an authentic, responsible self; firstly, by imposing a dualistic pattern upon it and, secondly, by insisting that the meaning of life was to be found outside in some alternative world.

But for Ursula religion functions in an entirely different way. She has no interest in it, in so far as it lays down rules and regulations for the organization of life. She senses instinctively how these can stifle the growing self. She is attracted to those dimensions of religion where language is used imaginatively and non-literally. Those great Eastern symbolic expressions, whose meanings can neither be fully grasped nor interpreted, are what interest her. They allow the self to grow without wholly defining it. Religion thus understood protects the dark forest, drawing it forth without prescribing fixed bounds for it.

This idea that there is something in human experience which is radically mysterious Lawrence shares with some Continental thinkers I have mentioned. Jaspers, with his own concept of 'the encompassing' in mind and writing about Nietzsche and Kierkegaard, notes how 'both questioned reason from the depths of *Existenz*'; how they brought forth no doctrines, no picture of the world, but rather created a totally new intellectual attitude for men in which reflection was now conscious of being unable to attain any real ground by itself; how Kierkegaard was astonished at those learned professors of science who never '. . . experience the maturity of that critical point where everything turns upside down, where one understands more and more that there is something which one cannot understand'.[35] And he goes on to note how both recognized that such an experience was incapable of direct expression and so both became philosophers with masks expressing themselves in *signa*, 'which do not connote what is meant but are themselves capable of endless explication'.[36] This dimension of human experience Jaspers calls 'the encompassing' and it can only be expressed in cyphers or symbols.

Lawrence himself explores this dimension more fully in his essay 'Hymns in a Man's Life'. Here he recalls names and images from hymns learned as a boy, which were never fully understood and were the better for this. *Studies* examined the way in which scientific knowledge with its tiresome enumeration of phenomena and its claim to completeness could halt that extension of human consciousness which was the purpose of life. Though he notes, in passing, that genuine science makes no such claims and involves a similar extension. The images from the old hymns have kept alive for him a sense of wonder and therefore areas of new and unexpected growth for the self, which the closed systematic knowledge of modern science has tried to kill. When Lawrence speaks of 'a natural religious sense' it is of this sense of wonder, a perception of the radical mystery at the heart of any aspect of human experience:

> And by the religious faculty we mean the inward worship of the creative life-mystery: the implicit knowledge that life is unfathomable and unsearchable in its motives, not to be described, having no ascribable goal save the bringing-forth of an ever-changing ever-unfolding creation. . . . [37]

But he is aware now of what we noted in *Studies* as an essential precondition of such a view, namely that there should be more than one concept of what it means to know: 'Somebody says that mystery is nothing, because mystery is something you don't know, and what you don't know is nothing to you. But there is more than one way of knowing.'[38] It is in this way that religion works for Ursula. Her father in his arguments with Anna made the mistake of thinking that religious utterances had to pass the test of literal or scientific truth if his intellect and his emotions were to be allowed to respond to them. Ursula, however, sees no reason why religious language should be applied literally.[39] Her growing self, therefore, can never be imprisoned by it; on the other hand her 'non-literal' interpretations can sometimes be whimsical.

If religion, then, for Ursula is freed from its dogmatic, restricting influence, can we also say that it has lost its other-worldly characteristics, which tend to bring about an irresponsibility about this life? Here there are still grounds for hesitation. In one sense it is true, the importance of religion for Ursula lies in its positive effect on the quality of this life. It gives her a perspective outside the storm of babies and the general chaos of life in the Brangwen household from which she can evaluate and take effective action upon it; even if this action should involve removing herself from it. Unlike Anna she refuses to accept the *cul-de-sac* of the breeding mother and it is religion which, at this point, keeps alive the assurance of other possibilities within herself. Furthermore, the chaotic life itself is partly redeemed by the ritual associated with the Church's year – 'the epic of the soul of mankind' – which introduces some order into an otherwise 'ragged, inconsequential life'.[40]

Nevertheless, there remains a danger. When the religious sense – this feeling of wonder before the unfathomable or the unsearchable – is cut off from the moral sense, from daily, practical questions of right and wrong, of personal responsibility, there is always a tendency towards a contemplative, religious quietism. Even the most austere religious dogma can degenerate into mere aestheticism. And there is something of this in Ursula's musings on the Sons of God and the daughters of men; in her reflections on Jesus' admonition to poverty and her refusal to allow it mean anything in terms of what she or her family might actually do. Wittgenstein once remarked that language only has meaning in 'the stream of life'. Ursula's non-literal use of religious language is always in danger of losing contact with those forms of life where alone it can remain intelligible.

But the chapter concludes with a positive evocation of the Resurrection – a life of full adult growth in the flesh, free from the crippling influences of religious nostalgia and a rejection of any religious view in which 'heaven is impatient for me and bitter against this earth'. The importance of religious discourse is finally to be assessed by its capacity to provide a vision not of an alternative life but an enlarged and more perfect life here and now. Therefore Ursula concludes that the Resurrection is to life and not to death; that it means wholeness, integrity and a gladness in the flesh.[41] It is wholeness and totality here which is insisted upon.

Religion, then, is no longer understood merely as a source of spiritual dualism, nor of alienation. Rather the open texture of its language and imagery is seen as an effective defence against any quasi-scientific or utilitarian attempt to explain human nature and so confine it. This is a view of religion which Lawrence was to hold until the end of his life. It appears at the end in *Apocalypse* and in *A Propos of Lady Chatterley's Lover*. However, it never again plays a significant part in the major fiction. And some of the reasons for this are already implicit in what has been said. It is easy to see how religious language understood in this way can liberate man *from* any predetermined view of the self but it is more difficult to see what he is being liberated *for*. While Lawrence is aware, at least at times, that he is speaking about a form of knowledge which is different from scientific knowledge, but a form of *knowledge* none the less, he never develops sufficiently his view of the nature of this knowledge to show how to distinguish sense from nonsense in that sphere. *The Plumed Serpent* is a good example of such a failure. When Ursula speaks about a non-literal use of language it is easy to see what she is *not* speaking about but more difficult to say positively what she has in mind beyond merely letting words mean, and making them do, whatever she chooses.

It is therefore a useful and liberating mode of experience for Ursula to grow up in but it never becomes a central part of her adult experience. It prepares her by keeping her open and orientating her towards certain areas of growth, of which, in the end, it will form no significant part. As she expresses it later in discussions with Winifred Inger, 'all the religion she knew was but a particular clothing to a human aspiration'.[42] There is no indication here that the clothing can partly determine and structure the aspiration itself nor that some forms of clothing might be more adequate than others.

The affair with Anton Skrebensky is crucial in Ursula's quest for authentic selfhood and it will qualify everything that has happened to her so far. For through it she comes to accept – though with a touch of horror – dimensions of her self of whose existence she had not dreamed, the same dimensions from which Anna Brangwen had shrunk in dread. From one part of herself Ursula would prefer not to know about them either. Like Franklin and Crèvecoeur, she wants a self she can put in her pocket, one already contained within those forms which society has developed and which therefore society will accept. But she has an honesty beyond her mother and she accepts, if reluctantly, what is revealed to her in her passion for Skrebensky.

Her attitude, then, is ambivalent. At one level of her consciousness she wants a 'normal' relationship. She wants Skrebensky to contain her, to overcome in her those destructive feelings of which she is becoming aware. In the stackyard after the dance we are told, 'She was afraid of what she was'.[43] On the other hand she loves this new self, even while she fears it and she is fascinated by that cold obstinacy in herself which seeks to destroy Skrebensky and the inauthentic life for which he stands. As they embrace she allows this new destructive self to dominate her consciousness and she is shocked by what this reveals in her. But after a time the old social self begins to reassert itself and she wants to forget what has happened, to forget what she has seen. She is filled with a fear of herself and with a desire that this other corrosive self should not be.[44] She wants to insist now that she is 'good' and 'loving', as she tries to put the old Skrebensky together again. She wants to insist that she really has all the normal feelings which a young girl should have in such a situation. 'But the vision remains and she cannot renege on it. If maggots in a dead dog be but God kissing carrion, what then is not God?'[45] The veil of laws, customs and language by which man makes reality tolerable to himself has been torn and Ursula has glimpsed, for a moment, what lies behind it. It gives her a sinister sense of liberation which leads to the perverse relationship with Winifred Inger in the following chapter. In Nietzsche's phrase she has passed 'beyond good and evil', that is beyond any concept of good and evil a decadent European civilization would recognize or its concept of God represent.

She feels now that she has 'all licence'.[46] And while it is true that she has won a victory in terms of personal growth, nevertheless she has to learn that her new morality is not all licence, that the new self which has been revealed will impose its own laws.

This, I think, is the intention of the chapter 'Shame', in which Ursula attempts an affair with Winifred Inger which is beyond conventional morality and the self which it envisages. For Lawrence wants to note that even when Ursula resists the restrictions which dead social forms impose upon her she has still nature itself to reckon with and in the end she refuses 'to mingle with the perverted life of the elder woman'.[47] Perverted, because Winifred has no respect for nature itself and the point is reinforced when she is paired off with Tom Brangwen, another character who has denied his own nature and given it over to the machine.

Skrebensky himself wants a relationship with Ursula which his sense of duty and of social responsibility can contain. But this is not forthcoming. Ursula forces him to glimpse possibilities in himself which are antithetical to this sense of duty; to see dimensions of himself which must remain unfulfilled if he is to take on the role of the good citizen. He in turn cannot accept that the individual is so important and so he settles for a mode of life in which this other, dark self will remain wholly unrealized. But Ursula demands a greater freedom, demands to be liberated from the small restrictions of the social world which the relationship with Skrebensky imposes upon her.

She has now reached a crisis in the development of her self. She suffers 'all the anguish of youth's reaching for some unknown ideal, that it can't grasp, can't even distinguish or conceive'.[48] But whatever else the ideal involves it can only be achieved in freedom and independence. Furthermore this freedom cannot be conceived in a negative way only as freedom from the kind of restrictions which Skrebensky brings to her, but positively as freedom to act within that society to which he belongs. No longer can it flourish purely in her imagination with her musings on the Sons of God and the daughters of men, nor can it grow apart from the world in a merely private relationship. She sees as fatal any attempt to seek her fulfilment, as her mother had done, by isolating herself from the society of which she disapproves and attempting a purely private fulfilment. It is in the public world of action and thought that the self is created and grows. The dreamy ideals of the girl from Cossethay have to be tested and enlarged and her freedom achieved in 'the great world of responsible work'.[49] This confrontation was inevitable from the beginning of the book when the young men of the Marsh were orientated towards the larger social world 'to enlarge their scope and range and freedom'.[50] And it was also implicit in the concept of the self outlined in *Studies* when Lawrence observed that men were most free when they became an organic part of a living community.

But the self and society still retain their ambivalent relationship. Ursula does come to terms with this world but in order to do so she has to pay 'a great price out of her own soul'.[51] She gains independence, poise and control; she establishes herself in that social world where alone the future lies. Recalling her colleagues from St Philip's after she has left she muses:

> She felt she loved them all. They were her fellow-workers. She carried away from the school a pride she could never lose. She had her place as a comrade and a sharer in the work of the school, her fellow teachers had signed to her, as one of them. And she was one of the workers, she had put in her tiny brick to the fabric man was building, she had qualified herself as co-builder.[52]

This is the very antithesis of that blood-intimacy which continually frustrated her predecessors from attaining full freedom, which drove them back upon themselves, into the close family huddle which excluded the outside world. And if Ursula was to develop it was essential that she should become a sharer in such a world.

But the price she pays is high. She has taken 'a strong, cruel move towards freeing herself'.[53] She has gained her position by becoming less personal, more mechanical, in effect, more like the Mr Harbys and the Mr Blunts whom she despises. Apparently Ursula can achieve her social position only at the price of her individual self. The paradox seems intractable. For on the one hand we want to say that the individual self cannot be defined apart from its position in society and on the other it seems that the ideals of the self as social are wholly inimical to its ideals as personal. The authentic individual self is socially inauthentic while the authentic social self, as Ursula discovers, is only achieved in the sacrifice of some of its personal authenticity. The point which must be stressed and which Ursula has realized is that the contradiction cannot be avoided by withdrawing from the social world, because the form which a personal life takes will always be in part derived from and in part dependent upon the society within which they are necessarily situated. Mr Harby can argue, as his wife does, that he is merely creating conditions without which the kind of personal life to which Ursula aspires would not be possible.

It has been the hope of political philosophers since Hegel that the essential alienation which exists between the authentic individual and the good citizen is temporary and that it is the task of politics to create a society where the two will coincide. Lawrence did not share this hope and his attitude to politics, with the exception of a rather trite flirtation with it in *Kangaroo*, is uniformly negative. As a result he frequently invests social and political institutions with the same kind of in- evitability which he sees in natural phenomena. St Philip's school and the teaching methods of Mr Harby are presented as given data to which Ursula must conform if she is to take her place in the world of responsible work. The idea that there might be other types of educational institutions and other ways of teaching children, less mechanical and less destructive of the individual, is not mooted. It is not suggested that Ursula in finding and creating the social dimensions of her self might also have an obligation to change those institutions which are to become constitutive of the new self. Significantly she refuses to share Maggie Schofield's interest in politics, being unable to see any connection between her own inner desire for freedom and effective political action to create a society in which the cost of that freedom might be reduced.[54] This refusal is linked with 'her passionate know- ledge of religion' and so underlines the point already made about the weakness of this concept in its failure to engage in any public mode of shared experience.

The point, however, should not be over-stressed. It is true that we can imagine educational institutions and methods of teaching which are less personally inauthentic than those which Ursula finds at St Philip's. More generally we can imagine social and political changes which would make the life of the individual in society more human. And since the individual self can only attain its freedom as a part of living community then the quest for personal fulfilment must include an obligation to assist in the construction of a community whose institutions are created by and are always revised in the light of purposes which are strictly human. Nevertheless the idea of a society in which the authentic individual and the good citizen are identical remains Utopian. And the idea that the contradictions of the human situation can be wholly eradicated by social reform is facile. Furthermore, if we link this chapter with the earlier one which described Ursula's affair with Skrebensky and if we note those disturbing and destructive dimensions of the self revealed there – the dark forest of *Studies* – we are surely confronting a reality with which no political theory can cope. And here of course is the heart of Lawrence's disenchantment with politics. The scientific pretensions of contemporary politics, with its roots in 'sciences' like sociology and economics, are congenitally incapable of grasping those dimensions of the human personality upon which Lawrence sets such store. In other words Ursula's revulsion from politics is merely another expression of Lawrence's own revulsion from any project or method of understanding which would nail down the self and so shut it off from the freedom and the responsibility of 'the open road'.

However, the open road and the extension of consciousness which it implies involves Ursula in the initiation into the larger community which she achieves at St Philip's with the degree of self-destruction which that entails. The experience has so seared her soul that she is tempted for a time to go back and seek the old life of personal intimacy. This temptation is strongest in the presence of Maggie Schofield's brother, the gardener. Here she is made more aware of the price she has paid for her place in the great world of responsible work. 'Oh, I love it. What more does one want than to live in this beautiful place, and make things grow in your garden? It is like the Garden of Eden.'[55] But Eden is lost and, though the desire to recapture it is strong with Ursula, as it was with Lawrence, it is to be resisted for it can only offer a mould for the self which is old, static and complete, as Melville discovered. Ursula is 'a traveller on the face of the earth', and Anthony Schofield 'an isolated creature living in the fulfilment of his own senses'.[56] In an essay in 1924 Lawrence produced his definition of man as 'a thought adventurer'[57] and it is under such a definition that Ursula is to be understood here. She is like Lou Witt at the end of *St Mawr*, who, in spite of her profound dissatisfaction with contemporary civilization and her fascination for the primitive life represented by the stallion St Mawr, sees nevertheless that the future lies not in going back but forward to a higher, more vital sense of civilized life:

For all savagery is half-sordid. And man is only himself when he is fighting on and on, to overcome the sordidness.

And every civilization, when it loses its inward vision and its cleaner energy, falls into a new sort of sordidness, more vast and more stupendous than the old savage sort. An Augean stables of metallic filth.

And all the time, man has to rouse himself afresh, to cleanse the new accumulations of refuse. To win from the crude wild nature a victory and the power to make another start, and to cleanse behind him the century deep deposits of layer upon layer of refuse: even of tin cans.[58]

Ursula too must go on and on, we are told, 'seeking the goal that she knew she did draw nearer to'.[59] And the way is not back behind civilization but forward and through it. We are once again reminded of Nietzsche whose philosophy too was thought to contain a kind of naturalism but who was at pains, as we shall see later, to distinguish his naturalism from that of Rousseau.

Progress in my sense. – I too speak of a 'return to nature', although it is not really a going back but a *going up* – up into a high, free, even frightful nature and naturalness, such as plays with great tasks, is *permitted* to play with them.[60]

And in her affair with Skrebensky Ursula, too, discovered something in her nature which was 'frightful'.

The presentation of Ursula's initiation into college life, from her initial sense of awe to one of increasing contempt, is well done. Few can fail to recognize in this picture the bankruptcy of much of what passes for education. Ursula is idealistic and comes to college thinking of it as a 'religious retreat' but finds instead nothing but a 'a little, slovenly laboratory for the factory' and the other commercial interests of the town.[61] It is nothing but a second-hand shop where one buys equipment for examinations. But with Lawrence's criticism is mingled a sense of deepening depression in which the voice of the moralist sometimes sounds above that of the artist. Ursula's teaching experience at St Philip's was presented with great subtlety and the tension between the damage she suffered there and her need to be there to gain freedom and maturity carefully sustained. Here, however, there is a lapse and Lawrence's attitude towards the college and all that it teaches and represents (with the unique exception of biology and for reasons which have little to do with the stated objectives of biology) is wholly negative. The college is nothing but 'a little apprentice-shop where one was further equipped for making money'.[62] Chaucer is spurious, the study of French is spurious, the study of Latin is spurious and this pessimism widens till we are told: 'Everywhere, everything was debased to the same service. Everything went to produce vulgar things, to encumber material life.'[63] And from this he moves to the powerful image of the circle lighted by the lamp – 'by man's completest consciousness' – and the darkness beyond where one could just glimpse the eyes of wild beasts – the dark forest again:

> Yea, and no man dared even throw a firebrand into the darkness. For if he did he was jeered to death by the others, who cried 'Fool, anti-social knave, why would you disturb us with bogeys? There *is* no darkness. We move and live and have our being within the light, and unto us is given the eternal light of knowledge, we comprise and comprehend the innermost core and issue of knowledge. Fool and knave, how dare you belittle us with the darkness?'[64]

Knowing how sensitive Lawrence was to the jeering we can begin to hear in the application of this symbol – though not in the symbol itself – the voice of the snubbed Messiah. For the spurious Chaucer has thrown his firebrand too as have many others whose testimony to the dark was preserved – albeit unwittingly – by unworthy ministers like those at Nottingham. It is not the criticism of bogus standards of excellence based upon a limited vision of man and the world, nor his battle for the recovery of the dark forest, which is the difficulty here. It is his failure, at this point, to preserve the tension required to make the relevant discriminations within the world of culture and to see the way in which those excursions into the dark are human projects also and a part 'of man's onward-struggle towards further creation'.[65]

And the discrimination does fail when Ursula comes to include everything within the scope of her pessimism.

She drops her French to study biology because in 'the strange laws of the vegetable world' she has 'a glimpse of something working entirely apart from the purpose of the human world'.[66] And so, almost in exasperation it seems, Ursula, and, I think, Lawrence, surrenders the word 'human' to those purposes within the human world which are mechanical and depersonalizing. Indeed, she surrenders it to all those things which we would like to say were least *human* in our social life.

Ursula's disillusionment with the college has another source and it is one we have come to recognize. Her original expectations were coloured by her idea of it as a place of religious retreat where the lecturers were seen as priests and where knowledge was imparted 'within the shadow of religion'.[67] Against such expectations the idea that a college education might help the student to a job in which he might attain a better standard of living is bound to seem tawdry, sinful even. It is another example of how a romantic idealism can place impossible demands upon the reality it is supposed to interpret. But more than this, we have already noted the essential impracticality of Ursula's concept of religion. Religious language and religious experience were for her insulated from the public world of everyday actions and duties. Once the educational processes of the college are conceived in religious terms, therefore, the impracticality becomes inevitable. The pursuit of knowledge as a religious task means the pursuit of knowledge, purely for its own sake. The dilemma, therefore, of the intrinsic aims of education as initiation into knowledge and understanding and of any extrinsic aims which schooling may have, is insurmountable. Lawrence is rightly trying to affirm the value of disinterested knowledge in a society whose values are almost wholly commercial. But the value of such an affirmation is diminished when the ideal of learning evoked is so entirely cut off from the actual community in which the self is seeking its growth.

But Ursula's growing dissatisfaction with the social world and the world of culture and in particular her perception of the mechanical life it creates in its exclusion of the dark forest, sends her back to Skrebensky to seek again that larger self which she glimpsed with him before. But she meets with the same failure as before and he only underlines the unproductive dichotomy between the individual and the social self. At first, it is true, while he is on holiday he can temporarily slough his public self as together they set themselves up in opposition to the ordinary life of society, so that they manage to achieve 'their final entry into the source of creation'.[68] But Skrebensky cannot maintain such a form of life. In him the sharp distinction between the personal and the social self is complete and he belongs to the latter. So Ursula feels that he has nothing to do with 'her permanent self' which she contrasts with 'her temporal, social self'.[69] The Skrebensky to whom she responds is someone she has created herself, while the real Skrebensky is as dead, mechanical and wooden as every other social artefact against which she is now in revolt. For 'in her, the antagonism to the social imposition was for the time complete and final'.[70]

It is when Skrebensky suggests marriage that the impossibility of their relationship finally begins to emerge. For marriage is crucial since it is the form in which the explorers of the dark forest present themselves to society and are placed and understood by it. As soon as he even thinks of marriage, Skrebensky is forced to try to see their relationship in its social context. Married, he will have to assume again his social self; they will be Mr and Mrs Skrebensky with all the social relationships which that implies and in turn society will understand them; it will place them and define them. And Ursula is now convinced that any social relationship – at least any she knows or can imagine – will cut her off finally from that freedom towards which she aspired when first she left home to take her place in the responsible world of work, a world, incidentally, of which she now seems to have despaired. In her illness at the end of the book, she repeats over and over to herself:

> I have no father nor mother nor lover, I have no allocated place in the world of things, I do not belong to Beldover nor to Nottingham nor to England nor to this world, they none of them exist, I am trammelled and entangled in them, but they are all unreal. I must break out of it, like a nut from its shell which is an unreality.[71]

All the relationships she has known have now become prisons of the spirit. They cut off her access to the open road, turning the self into a deformed, ugly, mechanical puppet. Thus, though tempted to the very end, as when she feels that she should simply have 'her man, her children, her place of shelter under the sun' and when she declares that her mother had been 'simple and radically true',[72] nevertheless she refuses them all and remains open. Still lacking, however, is any positive relationship with the community which is essential if her freedom is to become a reality. She tells of all the things, people, places and institutions to which she does not belong, but where is that 'living, organic, believing community' within which the full potential of the self, individual and social, can become actual? It is surely not without significance that this book marks the beginning of Lawrence's drifting from one country to another and of his abortive attempts to found little Utopias with different groups of friends.

The view of the self given in *The Rainbow* is remarkable in its complexity and sophistication. The major advance on the earlier novels is in Lawrence's clear perception of the social dimensions of the self and in his efforts to define the subtle relationships between these and the aspirations of its characters towards personal authenticity and freedom. This new dimension is seen at the outset when the women of the Marsh feel the need to turn away from the personal blood-intimacy of their life there to a higher stage of man's enterprise at civilization. It is seen again in Will Brangwen's failure to achieve an integrated self through his inability to find a living articulation for his aspirations, sustained and vitalized within an appropriate form of social life. In no other activity is the social infrastructure of the self so clearly revealed as it is in the use of language. And finally it is seen in Ursula's realization that the search for freedom must take her into 'the great world of responsible work'.

Most of the tensions of the later parts of the book arise from Ursula's attempts to acquire the relevant social infrastructure for the self while, at the same time, she tries to retain an authentic relationship with the apparently antisocial tendencies of the blood-consciousness. Some of the most disturbing, and the most successful parts occur in the revelation of those areas of the self which belong to the dark forest of *Studies* and which seem to challenge all our attempts either to define human nature or to make it manageable. By throwing his firebrands into the dark, Lawrence provides insights which cause us to question the adequacy of our social institutions for the growth or development of the self. More than this, he makes us ask whether in certain of its aspects the self should be allowed to develop at all. But while the limitations of society, education and culture are exposed, they are nevertheless seen – apart from those passages in the concluding chapters already noted – as essential constituents in an integrated life.

In *Women in Love* Lawrence will return to these problems and, while retaining his view of the central role which society and culture must play in the life of the individual, will analyse with increasing care the different ways in which both can become impediments to personal authenticity. He will try once again to define the relationship between the self as given in Nature on the one hand and as a product of society, culture and language on the other.

5 Culture, Art and Language: *Women in Love*

In *Women in Love* the structures of the self, its conditions of growth and disintegration, are essentially the same as those found in *Studies* and in the earlier novels. However the sources of disintegration in culture and society are identified differently and the novel has an altogether more contemporary conception of the problems of being human. (Indeed those ideals designated by the word 'human' are themselves called in question as adequate aims for the aspiring self in a way which recalls the title of Nietzsche's *Human, All-Too-Human.*) Dangers to the self only hinted at in the earlier novels are fully explored here. For example that condition represented by the cultured mistress of Alfred Brangwen, that 'inhuman being who used up human life for cold, unliving purposes',[1] is much more fully investigated in the person of Hermione Roddice, just as the industrial magnate, first seen in Ursula's uncle Tom, is expanded and deepened in the person of Gerald Crich.

In the earlier novels dualism emerged as one of the major obstacles in the path of the developing self; in particular that form of quasi-platonic dualism fostered by certain religious ideals, which denied the body and its desires in the interests of the spiritual soul. This form of puritanism is particularly evident in *Sons and Lovers* and in *The Scarlet Letter* and is identified by Lawrence as a mode of being which makes personal integrity impossible. In *Women in Love* dualism is still a crippling impediment in the life of the developing self but religion is no longer seen as an important instrument in fostering this condition. For Lawrence now finds the most dangerous origins of dualism in the culture-philistinism of Hermione on the one hand and in the industrial mentality of Gerald on the other. It may well be that the nineteenth-century puritan ethic provided a suitable breeding ground for the dualism inherent in the industrial mentality but from our point of view it is more important to note the similarities between the idea of the self implied by religious dualism on the one hand and by the concept of an industrialized humanity on the other. It was the perception of these similarities which caused Gerald Vann to note that, while industrialism was 'the root of our modern irreverence' the concept of Nature which it implied was no different from that of the dualist predecessors of Thomas Aquinas and Albert the Great:

> We have come to a view of creatures very similar to that of the predecessors of Albert and Thomas, inasmuch as we are apt to regard them as mere means. But the end to which we relate them is entirely different. It is not God who makes them sink into insignificance; it is progress in the sense in which the word is usually understood, it is the Satan of efficiency, the fetish of purchasing power. Ultimately the end is utilitarian, of the baser sort of utilitarianism.[2]

We can see in Gerald Crich that 'Satan of efficiency' of which Gerald Vann speaks, though the idea that the motive force behind him is simply the fetish of purchasing-power would be a little too simple.

That decadence which Gerald and Hermione and some of the minor characters in the book embody is important when we come to specify the positive concept of the self which Birkin tries to define. For often, as Gerald points out, he appears to talk pure nonsense.[3] But at other times generalizations which appear wild and extravagant become insightful and pointed when they are viewed against the life-styles represented by Shortlands and Breadalby.

The social dimensions of the self insisted upon in *Studies* and in *The Rainbow* are still peremptory. However English society in the closing chapters of *The Rainbow* and in the whole of *Women in Love* is seen as irredeemably corrupt and wholly incapable of providing those conditions either of employment or social intercourse where an authentic self could develop. This dilemma is responsible for much of the pessimism in the book. The hostility with which Birkin regards English society is critical for one who holds, as Lawrence does, that the growth of the self is dependent upon its ability to exist as a part of a living, believing community. It was this analysis of the self as dependent upon society and at the same time threatened by it in all its known forms, which was at back of Lawrence's attempts to found the Utopian community of Radamin.

In trying, therefore, to specify the positive concept of the self which the novel offers it is important to analyse those modes of decadence which are revealed as the crucial weakness of English society. Hermione Roddice and the society to which she belongs embody one such mode.

In her earlier appearances in the novel Hermione presents quite promising possibilities. She is a highly cultured person and yet, as she shows in her conversation with Birkin in the classroom, she is critical of education when it places too much emphasis on consciousness and knowledge. Children, she believes, are diminished by being stimulated to consciousness; in acquiring knowledge they pull things to pieces and lose the sense of their wholeness. They lose the capacity for natural, spontaneous action and would be better like animals with no minds at all.[4] From her position as a representative of high culture these sentiments might seem to get the balance right. For cultured and educated though she is, they show that she is alert to the incipient dangers of the intellectual life and that she values the natural spontaneity of life and the wholeness of experience, both of which rank highly in Lawrence's own hierarchy of values.

But the novel shows us something quite different, firstly through Birkin's tirade against her in the classroom. To him Hermione is a sham. Her advocacy of instinct and spontaneity is hypocrisy and she never gives up her commitment to the very intellectualism she is here reviling. Knowing is everything to her, it is her whole life. 'You don't want to be an animal, you want to observe your own animal functions, to get a mental thrill out of them. . . . It all takes place in your head, under that skull of yours.'[5]

'It all takes place in your head.' This is the 'sex in the head' syndrome which Lawrence has described elsewhere. The phrase itself is compelling, but divested of its spatial characteristics (as it must be; it has nothing to do with physiology) what does it mean? How can bodily instincts be transferred to the head? Some light, I think, can be thrown on this idea if we look at what G. E. Moore presents as 'the ultimate and fundamental truth of Moral Philosophy':

> By far the most valuable things which we know or can imagine, are certain states of consciousness, which may be roughly described as the pleasures of human intercourse and the enjoyment of beautiful objects.[6]

Remembering the dominant position held by Moore in promulgating the philosophy of Bloomsbury and the close connection between Bloomsbury and the life-style which Lawrence gives us as Breadalby it will be no surprise to find in Moore an abstract formulation of those very principles which Birkin is here criticizing in Hermione.

What is wrong with Moore's statement is that it places the criterion of value on internal states of consciousness and those states are made to intrude between the individual and his action or more generally between the individual and the world. Whoever follows Moore's maxim is less concerned with what he is doing than with the states of consciousness which these produce in himself. This is the kind of action which Lawrence saw turning even heterosexual encounters into forms of masturbation where the other person becomes simply the occasion of my own sensations. It is the quest for such states of consciousness which is the continuing motive force of Hermione's action. That is why Birkin accuses her of pornography, of refusing to be conscious of what she really is. For Hermione always sees herself, as it were, from outside and interprets her action in the light of some preconceived impression. Hence her little scene at the door in Breadalby when the two Brangwens arrive: 'The two girls were embarrassed because she would not move into the house, but must have her little scene of welcome there on the path. The servants waited.'[7] There is no warm spontaneity here; Hermione is not a hostess welcoming two guests; she is someone playing the part of a hostess welcoming two guests. Everything in her life, Birkin suggests, is done with this bogus objectivity. It is as though she was always seeing herself as a protagonist in a romantic novel.

All Hermione's experiences are processed through 'states of consciousness' which impose patterns upon them and produce those 'papier-mâché realized selves' to which Birkin refers at the close of the chapter.[8] Her actions are monitored by states of consciousness and so are structured by cultural forms, already complete and therefore dead, which are the images of her chosen self. She is confined within those forms and the dark forest is stifled. It is scarcely necessary to note that Hermione here is a victim of Sartre's *mauvaise foi*.

But Hermione is also a very complex character. Beneath the surface of the little picture-show which is her life there is another, unacknowledged self insidiously corroding her ideals and all those forms to which she tries to subdue her experience. We see it, for instance, in the scene with the lapis-lazuli, never again adverted to by Hermione because nothing in her chosen conception of herself could help her interpret it. Birkin knows of this other self and because of his knowledge: '. . . he would never, never dare to break her will, and let loose the maelstrom of her subconscious, and see her in her ultimate madness.'[9] We see this other self most carefully exposed in the chapter called 'Woman to Woman'.

Most of the time Hermione exists purely at the level of her chosen cultured self; this is the world of her 'extant consciousness'. She is what she chooses to be. 'Her self was all in her head:'[10] But as the maxim from *Studies* reminds us, we are not the great choosers we think we are. There is something in Nature which can resist the categories we prescribe for it, and what is worse, that inner residual self will turn destructive if we try to stifle it within some set of wooden categories. This is what Hermione has attempted; the cultured self in her head is one thing:

> But there was a devastating cynicism at the bottom of her. She did not believe in her own universals – they were sham. She did not believe in the inner life – it was a trick, not a reality. She did not believe in the spiritual world – it was an affectation.[11]

She belongs to a cultured world which is completed and therefore dead; the gaps which should have allowed creative life to continue have been closed. Like so many of those contemporary novels of which Lawrence complained that they were mere imitations of other novels, so the life to which Hermione and her set aspire is merely an imitation of other lives. They play at being intellectuals, play at being cultured and even play at being spontaneous. We see Gudrun and Loerke indulge in the same kind of games at the end of the book. But the self identity which Hermione treasures is a construct of divergent elements drawn from a culture which for her has ceased to be creative. But somewhere in her nature she knows all this and hence her devastating cynicism – her final rejection of the culture to which her chosen self belongs. At bottom her attitude to culture and to that form of civilized life which on the surface she represents is more destructive even than Birkin's, who is an explicit critic of it. For with Birkin there is a 'final tolerance' through which he still values elements in the culture he reviles. Thus when, having listened to Birkin and Hermione discuss aesthetics and the Italian national consciousness, Ursula declares that they are both 'people of the same old tradition, the same withered deadening culture',[12] she is saying nothing which they do not in their separate ways know. The difference is that since Birkin knows it consciously he has the possibility of coming through it to a higher integrated self while Hermione, unable to face the consequences of her own cynicism, maintains within herself two mutually destructive principles. Her criticism, therefore, of that education which stimulates to consciousness has its purpose though it is a regressive one. As Lawrence expresses it elsewhere:

> The struggle for verbal consciousness should not be left out of art. It is a very great part of life. It is not superimposition of a theory. It is the passionate struggle into conscious being.[13]

Birkin is prepared to undertake this passionate struggle into consciousness while Hermione, for all her worship at the shrine of knowledge, is
not. As a representative of culture Hermione fears 'the life that leaps and
bounds into our limbs and our consciousness from out of the original
dark forest within us',[14] while from the dark she jeers at that little area
'lit up by man's completest consciousness'.

Gerald Crich is a different embodiment of the same dualism. He is first
shown to us at Shortlands as an advocate of all those conventions which
are, for him, not just the symbols but the very conditions of civilized life.
He does not approve of the unconventional behaviour of the bride and
groom at the church. People must not be allowed to do as they like; they
must be prepared to accept certain standards and certain conventions.
For if everyone did act spontaneously doing the individual thing, 'we
should have everybody cutting everybody's throat in five minutes'.[15]
This adherence to convention with the desire for the kind of order which
it implies reveals a certain uneasiness in Gerald which Birkin detects
when he remarks that he must have 'a nasty view of things'. For Gerald
does have a nasty view of things and in his own case at least not without
justification. As he presides over the traditions of Shortlands during his
father's illness he tries to embody the values he advocates here.

At one level of his consciousness, therefore, Gerald's desire for order
and control, like Hermione's espousal of culture, is strong. We see it in
his treatment of the Arab mare at the railway crossing. When Ursula
describes his behaviour as pointless and cruel, Gerald argues that the
horse is there for his use, that this is part of 'the natural order' and that if
the will of man does not dominate the instincts of the horse then the
horse will master him. Unlike Ursula, Gudrun is fascinated by Gerald's
capacity to subdue and dominate the frenzied instincts of the animal,
seeing in it his wider control over the whole chaos of instinctive life.
Physical life is somehow impure while life dominated by the mind is
clean, purged of all impurities.

The same desire for this ideal of order shows itself in his work in the
mines. His task here is 'to put his philosophy into practice by forcing
order into the established world'.[16] And by order Gerald means that the
mines should become the perfect reflection of his own mechanical will.
They will be run with a smooth efficiency in which everything and
everybody must play their part and be defined by their part. The
sentimental humanism of his father, which had retained men out of
compassion even when they had ceased to perform any useful task in the
running of the machine, was finished. Just as the horse was there for his
use and his body was there for his use, so too the people in the mines were

there for his use also; it was a part of 'the natural order'. The world of the mines was the original chaos and Gerald the god who would turn it into cosmos. He sees his task as a battle between his will on the one hand and 'the Matter he had to subjugate' on the other. At first the miners resent the redefinition of themselves entailed by the process of mechanization but later they come to prefer it.

> Their hearts died within them but their souls were satisfied. It was what they wanted . . . . He was just ahead of them in giving them what they wanted, this participation in a great and perfect system that subjected life to pure mathematical principles. This was the sort of freedom, the sort they really wanted. It was the first great step in undoing, the first great phase of chaos, the substitution of the mechanical for the organic.[17]

The substitution of the mechanical for the organic principle is a new form of the dichotomy between the chosen self and the natural self. What is happening in the mines is that human nature itself is being redefined by a dominant intellect allied to the means of production which belong to an industrialized society. And it brings into focus the modern doubt as to whether it is still possible to maintain an idea of human nature at all. Lionel Trilling, commenting on a remark of Marx, writes:

> 'Let us assume *man* to be *man*, and his relation to the world a human one.' It is an astonishing thing to say: in no other epoch of history had it been felt necessary to make that assumption explicit . . . . 'Let us assume *man* to be *man*' means 'Let us assume man to be not a machine.'[18]

For it is this assumption which is denied in the functionalism of Gerald Crich and by the miners who eventually become content with the new nature being created for them. Lawrence himself, however, had no doubts; there is a human nature and it shows itself nowhere more clearly than in the destructiveness of modern life which arises from the attempt to deny it. There are certain things which you must not do to nature either in yourself or in the person of another. 'Let man only approach his own self with a deep respect.'[19] And this Gerald will not do because at bottom, like Hermione, he has a deep cynicism about human nature when it is not firmly under the control of custom and reason. He *has* 'a nasty view of things'. And so he is uneasy when he thinks that Birkin is endorsing that 'pure culture in sensation' represented by the African carving. 'You like the wrong things, Rupert,' he tells him, 'things against yourself.'[20] For that kind of culture, culture beyond the control of the mind, will only lead to chaos – 'everyone cutting everyone else's throat.' But the alternative view of nature is not so simple either and Lawrence knows it, as is shown in his continuing rejection of any simple idea of going back to nature. There is a striking resemblance between the predicament of Gerald Crich and that of Socrates as analysed by Nietzsche, another critic of the dominance of the rational principle.[21]

Nietzsche's essay on Socrates is interesting both in the similarities and in the differences between the philosopher's and the novelist's treatment of the same essential types of contemporary decadence. Socrates, though an historical character, is taken by Nietzsche because he is a perennial case of a type which had taken on alarming significance in the modern world. For Nietzsche any consideration of history which cannot become present was a waste of time.

In this essay Nietzsche looks first at the conventional judgement that Socrates, and Plato and Aristotle whom he inspired, mark the triumph of reason over superstition and prejudice. Like Gerald Crich, Socrates liked nothing better than an argument. He moved among his contemporaries probing, questioning them with his dialectic on judgements and decisions which they had hitherto made, without thinking, on instinct or custom. He was 'philosophical' in the popular sense of the word: his actions were never spontaneous, never, that is, based upon instinct or passion; they were always the product of the rational mind exercised in careful analytic pursuits. His life was ascetic and reason his rule to the extent that he claimed not to know how anyone *could* act against what his reason told him was the right course. Thus Socrates was the first advocate of a lucid, rational, scientific approach to human problems and he is the enemy of obscurantism, mythology, prejudice and religion. This is the traditional interpretation of the Socratic dialectic.

But a closer look, Nietzsche tells us, will show that this is a superficial view; it mistakes the cause for the effect, the symptom for the disease. The traditional judgement about Socrates must be reversed. 'I recognize Socrates and Plato,' he tells us, 'as symptoms of decay, as agents of the dissolution of Greece. . . .'[22] The flight to reason, which Socrates led, was not the further step of a people on the path of ascending life, it was a desperate last expedient of a people become insecure in its instincts.

Everywhere the instincts were in anarchy; everywhere people were about five steps from excess: the *monstrum in animo* was the universal danger. 'The instincts want to play the tyrant; we must devise a *counter-tyrant* who is stronger.'[23]

And the counter-tyrant was to be the will dominated exclusively by reason. The key to Socrates is to be found in his reply to the visitor who told him that he was 'a cave of every evil lust'. 'That is true,' replied Socrates, 'but I have become master of them all.' Socrates' secret with the Athenians was the same as Gerald's secret with the miners; he was one step ahead of them and able to give them what they wanted just before they realized it themselves. Both Socrates and Gerald were further gone in corruption than their contemporaries. Because in Greece the natural flow of life had become perverted the very instincts of the people had become destructive so that the only alternative was to become 'absurdly rational'. When Socrates appeared Greece had already ceased to be 'a living, organic, believing community' just as Lawrence thought England had at the beginning of the twentieth century and hence the fascination of Socrates and Gerald. And so Nietzsche's judgement of Greece and, by implication and for for him more seriously, of Germany and European culture in general at the close of the nineteenth century:

> The moralism of Greek philosophers from Plato downwards is pathologically conditioned: likewise their estimation of dialectics. Reason = virtue = happiness means merely: one must imitate Socrates and counter the dark desires by producing permanent *daylight* – the daylight of reason. One must be prudent, clear, bright at any cost: every yielding to the instincts, to the unconscious, leads *downwards*. . . .[24]

Thus Nietzsche and Lawrence are both agreed that the dominance of reason over passion and instinct, involving as it does the suppression of the natural self to a dead mechanical principle, is a sign of decadence. And each in his own way, too, recognizes that catastrophe in the cultural life of a people which makes the flight to reason so seductive. Even though Lawrence tells us that 'nothing that comes from the deep, passional soul . . . can be bad'[25] it is no longer a simple matter to discover this source because, as Birkin tells us, 'life isn't really right, at the source'.[26]

Therefore while both men recognize the sterility and the destructiveness of the tyranny of the rational principle, neither advocates any simple return to primitive naturalism. 'In times like these to have to rely on one's instincts is one fatality more.'[27] Thus although Nietzsche considers himself to be a natural philosopher, attacking the Church's morality as 'anti-natural morality', he is careful to point out that he is not using 'Nature' in any regressive sense; he is not, in Lawrence's terms, a 'renegade'. As we have seen therefore he gives special attention to Rousseau. His naturalism is of quite a different order and must never be understood as a going-back to Nature. Now both he and Lawrence have been accused of naturalism in the regressive sense. Nietzsche's *Übermensch* has frequently been misrepresented as a concept whose import it was to recommend a return to some form of barbarism, a return finally achieved in the person of Hitler, and Russell, as we saw, describing Lawrence's philosophy as 'a mystical philosophy of "blood"', claimed that it too 'led straight to Auschwitz'.[28] Neither Nietzsche nor Lawrence had any such idea in mind. And so here, when Nietzsche comes to represent his ideal, as we have seen, it is Goethe he evokes – 'the last German before whom I feel reverence'.[29]

> *Goethe* – not a German event but a European one: . . . What he aspired to was *totality*; he strove against the separation of reason, sensuality, feeling, will . . . he disciplined himself to a whole, he created himself . . . .[30]

Goethe is a key point of reference in Nietzsche from the earliest works to the last. For he is able to attack the culture of his day and at the same time refute any charge of simplistic naturalism by pointing to Goethe as his ideal of achieved spontaneity, a concept which brings us close to the positive ideal of the self implied in *Women in Love*. And in his aspiration to totality, his resistance against any tendency towards the separation of reason, sensuality etc, he also embodies that ideal of integrity which Lawrence so often evokes in his attack on dualism.

Thus, Nietzsche's attack on Socrates, with the positive values implicit in it, parallels fairly closely Lawrence's own estimation of the dangers represented by Gerald Crich. For *Women in Love* is concerned with those more general issues raised by Nietzsche and, since our concern is with the general structures of the self, we can quite properly use Nietzsche's paradigm as a point of reference. Thus, if we take Nietzsche's hint, we will see that while Gerald's destruction is brought about by the dominance of the rational principle, that dominance itself is accepted by Gerald through fear of the subterranean self which he glimpses from time to time and which he knows will cause such destruction if unleashed. And undoubtedly it is destructive. It is that 'reservoir of black emotion' which 'burst within him and swamped him' in his encounter with Gudrun at the picnic.[31] It issues too in that 'subterranean desire to let go, to fling away everything, and lapse into sheer unrestrained, brutal licentiousness'.[32] And he finds a perfect symbol for this self which he fears as he dives for his drowning sister in Willey Water:

> And do you know, when you are down there, it is so cold, actually, and so endless, so different really from what it is on top, so endless – you wonder how it is so many are alive, why we're up here.[33]

Gerald is always haunted by the thought that the rational, civilized world which he tries to create and inhabit is fragile and continually threatened. If we use Nietzsche's language here we can say that it is threatened by an instinctive life which has turned perverse. Gerald is certainly insecure in his instincts. And, if we go further with Nietzsche and see that this insecurity is not simply an individual phenomenon but a social and cultural one as well, we get a much better picture of the integrity of the social and individual self upon which Lawrence lays such stress.

Like Socrates then, when Gerald perceives the 'cave of evil lusts' he tries to master them by setting up the counter-tyrant, reason. But it cannot work because in the last analysis reason cannot function apart from desire and its efforts will either collapse or harness and pervert certain natural desires to its own purposes. With reason and will Gerald constructs and holds together the whole social order both in the mines and in his personal life. But divorced from the deep passional centres of life, they no longer serve any living purpose and so are continually threatened. This is what brings Gerald into those black fits of despair in which he feels that everything including his very self is caving in and that he is holding it up with his own hands.[34] His life is poisoned at the source, he rejects that source and then finds that it 'doesn't centre at all. It is artificially held together . . . .'[35] While his father lived he was able to feel that the order and stability he needed really did exist outside himself, independent of his own will. But it was artificially, not organic, and with his father's death, it died too and Gerald is left holding it up with his own hands:

> His father after all had stood for the living world for him. Whilst his

father lived Gerald was not responsible for the world. But now his father was passing away Gerald found himself exposed and unready before the storm of living . . . . He did not inherit an established order and a living idea. The whole unifying idea of mankind seemed to be dying with his father, the centralizing force which had held the whole together seemed to collapse with his father, the parts were ready to go asunder in terrible disintegration.[36]

'He did not inherit an established order and a living idea.' In his description of Gerald's father Lawrence has shown how the old ideas in which he had believed, had died and served only to confuse him in his dealings with the world. And so Gerald is not born into that living, believing community in which alone, Lawrence believed, a fully free and spontaneous self could develop. Instead he is born into a period of criticism and doubt in which the instincts themselves have become dangerous and so he fluctuates between a genuine fear of his natural self and an attempt to create a completely new one in which he finally cannot believe. And so like Hermione, his failure is a failure to achieve an integrated self. In him that desire for rationality, order and civilization can never come to terms with the 'reservoir of black emotion' which threatens to swamp him.

Of course, unlike Nietzsche's Socrates, Gerald is more than just a 'type'. Christopher Ricks notes something of this in his criticism of F. R. Leavis' analysis of the diver episode.

. . . The effect of Dr. Leavis's insistence upon the way in which 'the end is here prefigured' is to curtail the proper sadness, the sense that Gerald's clean swimming has in it still some possibility of a buoyant self-surrender, the sense that Gerald is not yet done-for, not yet his final self.[37]

Gerald as an existing individual overflows the categories of the type he represents. Thus, for instance, when Birkin contemplates the corpse of Gerald:

With head oddly lifted, like a man who draws his head back from an insult, half haughtily, he watched the cold, mute, material face . . . . It sent a shaft like ice through the heart of the living man. Cold, mute, material! Birkin remembered how once Gerald had clutched his hand with a warm momentaneous grip of final love. For one second – then let go again, let go for ever.[38]

There is certainly a judgement here on the type of contemporary life which Gerald represented and which Birkin had resisted throughout the whole course of the novel. But the source of the pathos is the simple mourning of one friend for the death of another and for this the grip of the warm hand is sufficient without the metaphysics of 'final love' and all that it implies for Birkin in his understanding of the essential nature of human relationships. Such a response is only possible in the novel to the extent that Gerald has been created as an individual existing beyond the abstract categories which explain his tragedy. That Nietzsche should evoke a similar response in, say, a description of Plato's reaction to the death of Socrates is simply unthinkable.

Birkin is aware of the difficulties which Gerald and the others have inherited and he tries throughout the novel to create conditions and a form of life in which they can be overcome. He, too, sees that life has gone wrong 'at its source' and he is introduced in the novel as a critic of that culture in which the catastrophe has occurred. He appears, in other words, as an advocate of the individual or 'natural' self against the social. Against Gerald, who is arguing for the importance of standards and convention, Birkin maintains that one should do the individual thing and act spontaneously, though he recognizes, with Nietzsche, that in these times spontaneous action is difficult and perhaps even impossible. 'It is the hardest thing in the world,' he says, 'to act spontaneously.'[39] Nevertheless it is the ideal condition. He develops the point more fully in his conversation with Gerald in the train where he tells him that everything is completely bad, that we must smash up our present life because it has become like a skin or rind which is grown too tight, inhibiting further developments. It has become encrusted with the same dead culture that Thomas Crich inherited; it can only strangle the growing self and so must be destroyed.

The image of the rind and core Lawrence had already developed in 'The Crown'.[40] There the rind was identified with conventional morality and scientific rationalism. Conventional morality was nothing but a system of dead moulds, the leavings of older phases of the struggle into conscious being, which inevitably stifle the growing self. It is opposed to natural growth and must be overcome.

> Morality has usurped the Crown. The unborn, reacting upon the null walls of the womb, assumes that it has reached the limit of all space and all being. It concludes that its self is fulfilled, that all consummation is achieved. It takes for certain that itself has filled the whole of space and the whole of time.[41]

The idea of morality as something to be surpassed by a new morality of Nature has obvious points of contact with Nietzsche. But Lawrence goes on to show what he believes to be the effect of this imprisonment. When the individual sees that the morality which he accepts is incapable of providing possibilities for further developments and he is, nevertheless, incapable of abandoning it, he turns in upon himself to seek whatever satisfactions he can there. This is the source of the duality already noted in Gerald Crich. Thinking of marriage we are told, '. . . he would accept the established order in which he did not livingly believe, and then he would retreat to the underworld for his life'.[42] And the life which ensues is characterized by that process of reduction in sensation which Lawrence had analysed in the essay on Poe. It is the same sensationalism which he saw as disastrously characteristic of modern sexuality.

Scientific rationalism, being the dominant mode in which contemporary man has come to understand himself, has a similar deadening effect as it urges its own concepts upon him as a final description and explanation of himself and his world. It too closes the universe around us making us 'prisoner(s) within the walls of unliving facts'.[43] But in whatever form the rind appears, it must be broken up and destroyed before real creative life can begin again and so Birkin declares that until the whole order of society is smashed up, no proposals and no reforms will do any good.[44]

Now, while the image of the rind or core is helpful in revealing certain dangers of established moral systems or scientific world pictures, it can be misleading in presenting too simplistically the complex ways in which social and linguistic elements are constitutive of the infrastructure of the individual self. The individual self and the society in which it flourishes cannot be opposed in the simple way that this metaphor suggests. The confusion it generates often appears in the paradoxical positions which Birkin is forced to adopt. Here, for instance, where he is arguing that everything is completely bad, that our present life is like a tight skin which inhibits further growth and must be smashed up, the simple dualism of the rind image obscures the fact that Birkin, in his condemnation of contemporary life and culture, is speaking as a very sophisticated representative of that culture; that the values he evokes against our present life are in part derived from that life. As Nietzsche puts it:

. . . a condemnation of life by the living is after all no more than a symptom of a certain kind of life . . . . One would have to be situated *outside* life . . . to be permitted to touch upon the problem of the value of life at all.[45]

Just as we cannot speak outside language nor think outside thought, so we can find no point outside of life from which to judge the whole. As Ursula points out to Birkin later, with a stroke of healthy realism, 'After all, there *is* only the world.'[46]

The illusion of such an archimedean point, fostered by certain forms of religious thought, which encouraged a view of this life as an exile from another which was higher and better, was, Nietzsche believed, one of the chief sources of nineteenth-century pessimism. For belief in another world often disappeared without any adequate reappraisal of the attitude to this world which it had fostered. We noted elements of this in *Sons and Lovers* and remnants of it still remain in Birkin, contributing to those periods of black pessimism to which he is subject. Nevertheless Birkin is very much a part of the life and the culture which he wants to smash up. The individual is always more deeply involved and implicated in the society to which he belongs than the simple separation of the rind and core suggests. Rather as in the doctrine of original sin, the individual cannot set himself apart from the community's fault. And if society is to be regenerated it can only be regenerated from elements within it.

The idea of a purely natural self which could be opposed to a social one is, as we have seen, an illusion. But is Birkin advocating such an opposition?

Consider his position in the chapter 'An Island', where with this symbol of the island Lawrence gives him, at least for a moment, his impossible archimedean point from which he can slander mankind. Here he tells Ursula that he wants to see the world 'empty of people, just uninterrupted grass, and a hare sitting up . . . . Man is a mistake, he must go.'[47] And he goes on to say that he wants to give up his job because he no longer believes in that humanity of which he pretends to be a part. He wants, therefore, to break completely with the known social world. Gerald and Hermione, in their different ways, were destroyed by their involvement in it and Birkin seems to think here that the only way he can avoid a similar catastrophe is by cutting himself off completely from all forms of contemporary social life. But he cannot isolate himself from social life so easily. It is not just in our jobs that we are implicated in humanity. For even when he gives up his job he remains a user of a public language which is the structure of the shared experience of generations. This point is noted in passing when he tells Ursula that the word 'love' must be proscribed from human utterance for many years because it has become vulgarized and in turn vulgarizes those forms of life which it describes and determines. But, we wonder, is it only the word 'love' which must be so proscribed? Can any word be free of the taint of those public modes of life in which it plays a part? Birkin gives us to believe that by giving up his job and proscribing the word 'love', he can isolate himself from society and, seeing it as a whole, condemn it. There remain echoes in this condemnation of Schopenhauer's judgement on life as 'an episode unprofitably disturbing the blessed calm of nothingness'.[48] For what else, really, is his grass with the hare sitting up?

However, this is not the final word spoken in the chapter and it is certainly not the final position of the author of *Women in Love*. What gives these remarks here greater significance than similar ones in 'The Crown' or in other essays is the world of the novel in which they are placed. Birkin is not simply the mouthpiece for this strange philosophy; he is also a young man of the early twentieth century speaking to a young girl he finds attractive. The stark aphorism, 'man must go', is not unaffected by our being told later that the man who said it was '. . . beginning to feel a fool'.[49] In general Ursula provides the kick in the wind which Lawrence wanted introduced to the Platonic dialogues. Though we must remember that where Plato's concern is primarily the analysis of concepts, Lawrence's is with their reference to a lived experience. This is a matter of emphasis; neither task does, nor could, take place without the other. The total effect of what is said, therefore, is partly determined by the fact that Ursula is listening and remains unconvinced. In this way the metaphysic is made to 'subserve the artistic purpose beyond the artist's conscious aim'.[50]

Ursula senses the falseness in his attempt to isolate himself from that humanity of which he is so obviously a part. She hates his Messianic touch and his view is 'too picturesque and final'.[51] His rather romantic picture of the hare in the grass – certainly not an idea derived apart from that mankind which has been such a mistake – she ridicules. For this is 'a symptom of a certain kind of life'. And above all she notices in him a 'final tolerance' and in it a commitment to the very world he reviles.[52] The final impression, therefore, is more subtle than the simple presentation of the 'philosophy' suggests. Above all the chapter does not sustain the impression implicit in the image of the rind that there is a simple dualism between the social and the natural self, nor that the author is satisfied with Birkin's view that everything from society is bad and everything from nature unequivocally good.

Neither, of course, is Birkin satisfied with his own expression of his philosophy given here. The real complexity of his position can be seen in his attitude to language. Indeed it becomes increasingly apparent that the concept of the self outlined in *Studies* cannot be developed apart from an adequate theory of language. In a very real sense the problem of the self is the problem of language. This realization in no way trivializes the investigation. For what Wittgenstein says about mathematics is also true of language in general.

> I was asked in Cambridge whether I think that mathematics concerns ink marks on paper. I reply: in just the same sense in which chess concerns wooden figures. Chess, I mean, does not consist in pushing wooden figures around a board. If I say 'Now I will make myself a queen with very frightening eyes, she will drive everyone off the board' you will laugh. It does not matter what a pawn looks like. What is much rather the case is that the totality of rules of the game determines the logical place of a pawn. A pawn is a variable, like 'x' in logic.[53]

The study of language, then, is also a study of social and political institutions, of personal relations, etc, in which it plays a part. For neither can exist without the other. Just as in Wittgenstein's analogy a pawn is only a pawn within the rules of chess and without pawns, knights, bishops, etc there would be no chess. But most language games do not have the rigid rules and the closed contours of chess and mathematics and this difference gives rise to some of the problems which Lawrence experiences in his attempts to probe the relationship between the self and society. I shall investigate this problem more fully in this and in the two concluding chapters.

The problem of language was noticed first in *The Rainbow*. There we saw that human relationships always involved something more than could be said in language and that attempts to confine them within accepted forms of speech restricted and distorted them. On the other hand, failure to find the relevant articulation for our relationships left them incomplete and partly underrated. In Birkin this dilemma becomes conscious and is rendered explicit. He sees life in society as a threat to personal authenticity. While the self conceives its projects in the language of traditional morality which it finds in society, then it is doomed to be confined within the categories which belong to that morality. The culture-philistinism of Hermione, on its surface an alternative to the conventional, is no better and only provides an alternative orthodoxy, creating a self equally stereotyped and equally lifeless. Language, being a public activity, is the vehicle of personal inauthenticity. Hence his difficulties with the word 'love'. It has become tainted by its history. Indeed it cannot exist apart from its history and those forms of life in which it plays a part. In proscribing the word Birkin is either proscribing those forms of life to which it belongs or is seeking to alter them radically. Hence, he tells Ursula that he does not want a loving relationship with her but something beyond '. . . the emotional loving plane . . . where there is no speech and no terms of agreement'.[54] Only when it goes beyond speech can the self reach down to draw upon those resources from the dark forest where life 'bounds and leaps into our limbs and our consciousness'.[55]

On the other hand, Birkin does not accept the view that life can proceed solely on the level of the inarticulate. This was Tom Brangwen's mistake. It is not possible, and it would not be desirable, to regress to forms of human relationships which were completely independent of their expression in language. As the central instrument at the disposal of the developing self, language may have its dangers; but there is no other. And so in his relationship with Ursula, Birkin sees himself committed to seeking, however inadequately, the relevant articulation.

> There was always confusion in speech. Yet it must be spoken. Whichever way one moved, if one were to move forwards, one must break a way through. And to know, to give utterance, was to break a way through the walls of the prison as the infant in labour strives through the walls of the womb. There is no new movement now, without the breaking through of the old body, deliberately, in knowledge, in the struggle to get out.[56]

Here is the image of the rind again but language is no longer simply the dead husk, it is also the instrument used to break through it. It is not, as we have seen, a superstructure imposed upon life, but an essential part of the passionate struggle into conscious being. This underlines again the intrinsic continuity of the social and individual self. But how then can we avoid those forms of personal inauthenticity which occur when we try to contain the self within forms derived from a public language?

The fault surely does not lie in language at all but in a mistaken conception of it. It does not even lie with traditional morality but in a particular way of appropriating it. For, when the word 'love' first appeared as a cypher in human affairs, mankind took a step forward. And the same can be said of concepts like justice, temperance, courage, chastity. Things only start to go wrong when, seeing these concepts as complete and final, we try to coin the self with them. This happens when we accept a view of language in which words are seen as labels sticking on to or pointing to things already given in the world. What we must rather do is notice the way in which concepts are constitutive of those realities they seem merely to name. For instance, the 'things' we designate with the words 'husband' and 'wife' cannot exist before we have the concepts with which we represent them. For the relationship is not independent of the concepts in which we conceive it. And in so far as concepts belong to a living language and play a part in 'the stream of life' they can never be final and must change in the continuing struggle into conscious being. If words like 'love', 'justice', etc are not seen as 'open texture' words they do indeed become prisons of the self. For they are stages in the struggle into conscious being, not the end of the process. But as each stage is reached by the creative artist, like Lawrence *or* Plato and its language absorbed into a public mode of life, there is always the tendency for those who come after to take that expression as complete and to abandon the struggle. Any artist can be misunderstood and Lawrence too has been turned into a cult figure. For language is a public activity and will always enshrine and fossilize the values of the culture in which it is found. But it is more than this. It is an activity, a game, a creative project continually engendering new meanings and new significances. Nowhere is this process more evident than in the novel. The experience of *Women in Love* alters our use of concepts like love, culture, sex, art.

But however important language is, Lawrence still insists that there is something in human nature which goes beyond what can be said. Though it should be clear now that language itself can contain its own recognition of these limitations. Birkin tells Ursula,

> There is a final me which is stark and impersonal and beyond responsibility. So there is a final you. And it is there I would want to meet you . . . beyond, where there is no speech and no terms of agreement . . . Only there needs the pledge between us, that we will both cast off everything, cast off ourselves even, and cease to be, so that that which is perfectly ourselves can take place within us.[57]

It is here, Birkin believes, that Ursula must learn to trust herself and become 'glad and sure and indifferent'.[58] It will be a level at which she will not recognize her own existence, a form of life which her common self will deny.[59] But this surrender to the inner self is not a matter of viciousness or wantonness and is certainly not to be understood, as Ursula suggests, under the rubric of free love. No, Birkin tells her, in its demands the inner self is as imperious as any traditional morality. It must be approached with respect and this is why he insists there must be a bond or pledge. When Ursula says that he is merely reintroducing the old dead morality, he replies, 'No . . . it is the law of creation.'[60] And this rather anachronistic concept is at the centre of Lawrence's understanding of the relationship between man and the world. It entails a certain reverence for things which he found absent from contemporary life. It involves, too, something very like those '. . . laws of things which lie/Beyond the reach of human will and power'[61] of which Wordsworth spoke. So that when Ursula claims that Birkin has reverted to an old, dead morality his answer does not completely refute her claim. For his view does belong to an old tradition where the moral philosopher saw his task as the elucidation of those very laws of creation. Thus the criterion which Birkin is evoking here is certainly old, though it may not be dead.

He tells Ursula, therefore, that she must learn to trust herself, to let go so that that which is most perfectly herself can take place within her. But he does not mean by this that she should let herself go in any Dionysian ecstasy.[62] There are different ways of letting go. One way, we let go of everything commonplace and put ourselves into the power of those 'laws of things which lie/Beyond the reach of human will and power' and, in doing so, become glad, sure and indifferent. But there is another way of letting go in which, like Gerald we 'lapse into sheer unrestrained, brutal licentiousness', into that reservoir of black emotion. How, then, are we to distinguish these two? How are we to know those 'great desires that are fulfilled in long periods of time'[63] from others which are degenerate and corrupt? The problem is especially acute in a society which has become insecure in its instincts and, as Lawrence's evocation of life at Breadalby and Shortlands shows, it is of just such a society he is writing. Indeed, one sometimes feels that Gerald would like more than anything else to be able to tap the source of those great desires, but that he is so firmly fixed as a part of a degenerate society, partaking of its instincts and dispositions, that there is really nothing he can do about it. Once only in the book, as he returns from the picnic in the boat with Gudrun, does he seem to come near to a condition of being in which he too is subject to that law of creation: here his mind becomes submerged and he lapses out into the things around him.[64] But it is a rare moment for Gerald and ironically it is followed by the drowning for which he holds his own negligence responsible. Any further lapsing out is into that cold, insidious reality represented by the dark underwater of the pond. What, then, can be done when some instincts are creative, some perverse; when, as Nietzsche says, 'to have to rely on one's instincts is one fatality more'?

This is a question to which Lawrence returned many times. Generally, as in 'The Novel and the Feelings',[65] he believed that here again the novel had a great part to play. Since our civilization has been so destructive, especially where the natural flow of our sympathies is concerned, we can no longer rely upon the instincts, for there is no point in letting 'a whole rank tangle of liberated feeling spring up'. What we require instead is a cultivation of the feelings so that we can find again the old Adam. 'Not in viciousness nor in wantonness, but having God within the walls of himself.' We should learn to listen to 'the voices of the honourable beasts that call in the dark paths of the veins of our body, from the God in the heart'.[66] And if our civilization has so crippled us that we can no longer hear those voices in ourselves then we must 'look in the real novels, and there listen-in'.[67] In spite, therefore, of the primordial references to the old Adam and the dark forest, and the criticism of contemporary civilization, the regeneration of the natural self remains something inescapably culture-bound. Indeed it involves something not so very different from 'that very culture of the feelings' which John Stuart Mill discovered with all the force of a religious conversion when he first came upon the poems of Wordsworth.[68] And while it may not be possible to find a point outside tradition and culture from which to condemn the whole, it is possible and necessary to make relevant discriminations within it.

The significance of all this can be better appreciated and its logic more clearly defined if we look at the chapter 'A Chair', in which Birkin turns his attention directly onto the question of art and tradition. Here Ursula says, speaking of the chair which both she and Birkin have admired and bought:

> And I hate your past. I'm sick of it. . . . I believe I even hate that old chair, though it *is* beautiful. . . . I wish it had been smashed up when its day was over, not left to preach the beloved past to us. I'm sick of the beloved past.[69]

This would seem to say that the chair which belongs to the past is inimical to personal growth for that very reason; that while we have things from the past, even if they are beautifully finished works of art like the chair, we will belong to the past and it will imprison us, closing the open road and making further developments impossible. Lawrence himself sometimes becomes this very caricature of his own thought, as when he says in a letter in 1916 that 'because a thing *has been*, therefore, I will not fight for it'.[70] As though no idea which came from the past could nourish the present. For the cultural past which is embodied in art has the same stultifying effect upon the self as traditional morality had. But as with the earlier statement in 'An Island', the final impression of the chapter is subtler and more complex than this stark statement would suggest. For it is qualified by the discussion which follows and by the presence of the young man and woman, a couple who have little connection with the artistic tradition which enables Birkin and Ursula to admire the chair but who, nevertheless, hold a certain attraction for Ursula. Of the young man Lawrence says, 'He was a still, mindless creature, hardly a man at all, a creature that the towns have produced, strangely pure-bred and fine in one sense, furtive, quick, subtle.'[71] So different from Birkin and yet Birkin could never aspire to his condition without becoming renegade. Art and tradition may be damaging in one direction but there can be no going back because through them something significant is achieved. The contradiction in Ursula's remark itself opens up wider possibilities. The fact that the chair remains to 'tease us out of thought' represents its position in tradition in one direction only. In the admission that it was beautiful and had its day, much is already granted to tradition. For even in its day the chair owed much to earlier generations of craftsmen; it was creation made possible by a civilization in which an artistic tradition concerned with such things was allowed to develop and flourish.

And Birkin tries to define this more complex attitude to art and tradition as the chapter develops. There is, it is true, a kind of art – perhaps the bulk of what passes for art in our society – which has this crippling effect upon the present, burdening the developing consciousness with the completed forms of earlier generations. But this is only so of art offering itself as complete and finished. There is another kind which, while it continues to discriminate and to hold up what is best, can at the same time liberate and leave the future open. Birkin sees its paradigm in the works of Rodin and the later Michelangelo.

> You have to be like Rodin, Michael Angelo, and leave a piece of raw rock unfinished to your figure. You must leave your surroundings sketchy, unfinished, so that you are never contained, never confined, never dominated from the outside.[72]

They are achieved works of art which, in the language of *Studies*, continue to respect the dark forest and which express their own limitations in relation to their subject matter. The conception here is rather like Goethe's, who in speaking of his *Faust*, says,

> . . . the only matter of importance is, that the single masses (i.e. the individual parts of the work) should be clear and significant, while the

whole always remains incommensurable – and even on that account,
like an unsolved problem, constantly lures mankind to study it again
and again.[73]

In Goethe's formula, though the work is finished it is never exhausted in
any single explanation but is capable of endless explication. Birkin's
position is not significantly different from this and he is saying here of art
and tradition what has already been said of morality and language, that
its influence can be positive so long as it retains an open texture, but that
when it becomes closed and presents us with a vision which is final and
complete, it will confine and dominate and the open road will be closed.
And this is a focal point of reference in Lawrence's own criticism. It
leads him, for instance, to prefer Giovanni Verga over Dostoevsky
because Dostoevsky's characters always operate under some tyrannical
ideal of the self such as an ideal of life which encourages every shabby
little scrubber to think and to create for himself a unique, tender soul.
Whereas Verga's Don Gesualdo has only an outside; he lives his life
completely unaware of his own 'soul' and therefore of any idealized
picture of it. 'Not being under the tyrannical sway of the idea of "love",
he could be fond of his wife, and he could be fond of Diodata, and he
needn't get into a stew about any of them.'[74] Verga possesses what
Lawrence calls a Homeric quality; his characters are in a sense 'soul-
less'. Unlike Dostoevsky's characters they have no insides and it is this,
above all, which leaves Verga's works open like the late sculptures of
Michelangelo.

And any work of art, provided it is open-textured, even when it
belongs to the past, can be similarly creative and invigorating in the
present.

In *Women in Love* a quite different view of art is outlined by the
sculptor Loerke. For its value comes solely from its contemplation.
His first statement of his views appears quite promising. Telling Ursula
and Gudrun about a great granite frieze he is working on for a
factory in Cologne, he says that just as art used to interpret religion,
it must now interpret industry.[75] This would seem to fit well with
Birkin's formula about the artist creating a world that is fit to live in. For
since we live in an industrialized world it is important that the artist
should give meaning and significance to industry making its processes
more human, making our places of work places of beauty and of greater
humanity. But as we read on we find that this is not what the word
'interpret' means here at all. Art, according to Loerke, does not interpret
industry in the sense that it humanizes it. Rather industry through art

will mechanize man. '. . . machinery and the acts of labour,' he tells the girls, 'are extremely, maddeningly beautiful.' The frieze depicts a fair and, Loerke explains, at the fair the people enjoy the mechanical motion of their own bodies; they are serving the machine, enjoying its motion. For motion is everything.[76] And so motion and the sensation of motion become the only sources of value. Art is not interpreting industry in any creative sense, but human life through art is being interpreted and redefined *by* industry. It is the artistic counterpart of Gerald's attempt in the mines to subject life to pure, mathematical principles. For Loerke art has to be about sensations because there is nothing else. For he believes in nothing,[77] and is committed to nothing but his work. In his analysis of Loerke, Birkin shows his own commitment to the social ideal in art. Loerke, he tells Gerald, is a good many 'stages further in social hatred' than any of them:

> . . . He lives like a rat in the river of corruption, just where it falls over into the bottomless pit. He's farther on than we are. He hates the ideal more acutely. He *hates* the ideal utterly, yet it still dominates him . . . . He is a gnawing little negation, gnawing at the roots of life.[78]

In other words to attack the social principle is to attack life at its roots. This does not mean, of course, that society itself in whatever form it realizes the social principle is above criticism; it is merely another affirmation of the social dimension of the·individual self. Loerke, by aspiring to become a pure, individualized 'will', has renegued on those dimensions of his humanity which are essentially social. He and his art, Birkin is suggesting, have become the spearhead of that process of dehumanization upon which this novel is a recurring meditation.

As Loerke goes on to reveal himself we glimpse something of the degenerate life which is the counterpart of this theory of art. When he shows the sisters a picture of his sculpture of the young girl on the horse, Ursula attacks him for presenting the horse as something rigid and stiff. But he explains that he is not trying to create a picture of a friendly horse, that his horse is a piece of pure form, a part of a work of art which has 'no relation to anything outside the work of art'.[79] And when Ursula continues to press him saying that the stiff horse is really a picture of himself, he breaks into an angry defence of his work and of his theory of art. The work of art has no relation to anything outside itself; it is completely self-contained. To confound the everyday world and the world of art is to generate confusion.[80] This view of art, so diametrically opposed to Lawrence's own, is the perfect correlate of the utilitarian view of man, where the notion of good becomes identified with having sensations, the view which Lawrence parodied in the person of Hermione and which he criticized more abstractly in his essay on Poe. Art as pure form, with no acknowledged relation to any public form of life, must end in 'sensationalism', as Lawrence understands that word, and Loerke as its advocate has all the irresponsibility of a mere aesthete. Against this Ursula retorts with the Lawrentian view of art as essentially moral and as justified in its relation to lived experience. 'The world of art is the only truth about the real world,' she says.[81] The world of art and the world of life are not distinct planes of existence and the discussion of Loerke's statue which follows explores the conception of reality out of which the work was produced. For the sculpture does indeed reveal something of the sordid life of its creator – the well-known master-sculptor with his-young art student as mistress, the cruelty of his relationship with her culminating in his considered view that girls after the age of eighteen are no use to him. The view of life revealed here is not only anti-social but inhuman and as we have seen these are not contingent propositions. In short Loerke has a vision of the world, a view of life which is sordid and degrading and it shows itself in his art whether he likes it or not.

Art viewed objectively as mere form must subjectively be a matter of pure sensation and such a view was for Lawrence simply irresponsible and as Birkin has pointed out is grounded on a denial of the social dimension of the self. It is Loerke's hatred of the social ideal which turns him in on himself to construct a theory of art whose aim is the production through form of private sensations.

Lawrence's view of art, on the other hand, is essentially moral and social. But it is not didactic in the pejorative sense which this usually suggests. Art for art's sake, Nietzsche says, is an emotional reaction against moralizing in art. 'Rather no purpose at all than a moral purpose.' And the whole practice of *Studies in Classic American Literature* has shown how Lawrence too is sensitive to the damage done in art by a narrow view of morality. But, Nietzsche goes on, the rejection of a 'moral' purpose does not mean the rejection of all purpose in art: 'Is his basic instinct directed towards art, or is it not rather directed towards the meaning of art which is life? towards *a desideratum of life?*'[82] And Lawrence's best art is moral in just that sense i.e. in the sense in which morality is the 'science of life'. And this view of morality never becomes a narrow imposition so long as the art retains its open texture, while it remains, as Goethe says, like an unsolved problem constantly luring men to study it again and again. And therefore Birkin's original feelings about the chair, though qualified, remain true:

> When I see that clear, beautiful chair, and I think of England . . . it had living thoughts to unfold . . . and pure happiness in unfolding them. And now, we can only fish among the rubbish-heaps for the remnants of their old expression.[83]

Lawrence, then, is an advocate of culture and tradition so long as it is properly understood. And he frequently testifies to that community of which he feels himself a part: it includes Plato, Heraclitus, John the Evangelist, John of Patmos, Shakespeare, Keats and Wordsworth. But even while he does this he continues to worry about the great weight of the past and to declare that mankind has been a mistake. Viewed philosophically, these are contradictory positions, and sometimes in the letters and the non-fiction Lawrence does contradict himself. But in the novels they are placed in such a way as to become a part of an infinitely more complex attitude to the problems of tradition and art than anything in the non-fiction would lead us to suspect.

There is a sense in which the past through culture and tradition can stifle the growing self. This is always the case when its products are given as final and complete. Thomas Crich apprehended religion in that way, as Gerald did the forms of civilized behaviour which he inherited at Shortlands. Art, which is a part of the struggle into conscious being, becomes destructive when it puts an end to that struggle by offering its products as complete. The dummy self of Benjamin Franklin, whether it is given in philosophy, a novel, a painting or a scientific theory of man, is always a temptation to a nature which has grown tired of the uncertainty and the tensions of the struggle. And from time to time a form of life which is strange and enigmatic is repellent to all natures. But the closed alternative offers, as Sartre puts it, 'a character, a destiny, a means of escaping the inexhaustible gossip . . . of conscience'.[84]

There is, however, a different kind of art, a different way of relating to its traditions and this way corresponds to the open texture theory of language and together with it can provide an infrastructure for the self which keeps to the open road. With it the self is never 'contained, never confined, never dominated from the outside'.

The novel achieves this state when it is not an imitation of other novels, when the author escapes the dominance of some fixed idea or of some fixed form. And much, too, has to do with the way we read novels. For the most open-ended novelist – like Lawrence himself – can become a cult figure to whom others look for an identity which will put an end to the inexhaustible gossip of conscience. What Karl Jaspers says about the history of philosophy applies exactly to what we have been saying about art and the novel:

> . . . all appropriation of tradition proceeds from the intentness of our own life. The more determinedly I exist, as myself, within the conditions of the time the more clearly I shall hear the language of the past, the nearer I shall feel the glow of its life.[85]

And although Jaspers is thinking primarily of the moral or existential dimension of truth and of how to rescue it from objectivity, he is also thinking of the way in which the past can become a burden hampering us from attaining such truth. Indeed, when he goes on to speak of the dangers inherent in the study of philosophy it could be Lawrence speaking of Franklin again or of any of the old dead forms of knowing:

> Concepts which were originally reality pass through history as pieces of learning or information. What was once life becomes a pile of dead husks of concepts and these in turn become the subject of an objective history of philosophy.
>
> Everything depends therefore on encountering thought at its source . . . . Having been written down it can be rediscovered: at any time it can spark a new blaze.[86]

When Birkin endorses Ursula's criticism of the past, he seems to fear that the intentness of our lives, our capacity to exist determinedly within our own time is so diminished that the past can only be a pile of dead husks imposing upon us so that our knowledge of the past becomes 'objective' in the pejorative sense which Jaspers gives to that word: 'Knowledge that does not concern the knower comes between the content of knowledge and its resurrection.'[87] And it is with the resurrection of truth that Birkin is concerned, so that when he looks at the chair he knows it is not the past that is at fault, but our own feebleness in relation to it and therefore our incapacity to appropriate it as the living thought which it was.

In everything, then, that Lawrence has to say about art, morality, tradition and culture there operates as normative the same concept of the self he had developed in *Studies*. It it is a self which is embedded in nature and is also a construct of human language and thought. It therefore must belong to a community which shares a common tradition of culture and belief. However, within this community it must remain free, retaining a reverence for itself as a part of the created world. Finally, it must never identify itself with the intellectual principle. This had been the error of certain idealist philosophers and it is the error which is enshrined in the mechanical principle which dominates modern industrial society.

> For no part of us nor of our bodies shall be, which doth not feel religion: and let there be no lack of singing for the soul, no lack of leaping and dancing for the knees and heart; for all these know the gods.[88]

For all its modernity there is in *Women in Love* something of the Greek concept of tragedy which derives from the belief which Lawrence shares with the Greeks that, contrary to the view of most modern philosophers, there is a human nature and man ignores it at his peril. Like Prometheus, Gerald is punished when he disregards that law of creation of which Birkin spoke. He would become God himself, creating his own nature and the natures of the men who work for him; and this is *hubris* as the Greeks understood it.

But where the description of the self in *Studies* is abstract and general, in *Women in Love* this is translated into forms of contemporary life we can recognize. With Jaspers and the existentialists, Lawrence insists that 'knowledge is an experience, not a formula'[89] and it is in *Women in Love* that we are given the experience of the disintegrating self, destroyed by its attachment to forms of life which *Studies* indicated abstractly as ruinous. There too we are *involved* in that struggle into conscious being, the open road which *Studies* saw as 'the bravest doctrine man ever proposed to himself'.[90] The novel provides in effect 'that very culture of the feelings' essential to any theory of the self which stresses the importance of spontaneity and instinct in a society whose instincts themselves have become corrupt.

Furthermore, like the raw piece of unfinished rock of Michelangelo, the final impression of the novel is ambivalent. The central question of the relation between the social and the individual self is never solved. When Birkin and Ursula find themselves their first act is to resign their jobs, to retreat from 'the great world of responsible work'. And that community which was seen as essential to freedom is never found; Birkin's failure with Gerald is also his failure with the world and though Ursula thinks he should be content with *her*, he knows better. Freedom apart from the community is an illusion, as Ursula Brangwen saw in *The*

Rainbow when she first launched herself into the world of work. Birkin's dissatisfaction and the nature of the only community in which he could situate himself is pinpointed in a remark he makes to Gerald about young Winifred Crich and Gudrun. 'Only artists', he says, 'produce for each other the world that is fit to live in',[91] and the sense in which artists are the architects of the community is mystical. Nevertheless it is the only community to which Birkin and Lawrence finally belong. It is in effect a 'communion of saints' – though not of plaster saints – which while it can provide a meeting place where life can start to regenerate in a society wholly given over to corruption, can never create the concrete structures of that 'living, organic, believing community' in which alone freedom would be possible.

6 The Tyranny of the Phallic Consciousness: *Lady Chatterley's Lover*

. . . the metaphysic must always subserve the artistic purpose beyond the artist's conscious aim.

One of the major weaknesses of *Lady Chatterley's Lover* is that the metaphysic has been allowed to dominate. Lawrence becomes the victim of the very things the earlier novels and the criticism had warned against. The conceptual framework in which he understands the self is now fixed; its social infrastructure is no longer taken seriously and the only concepts of language which the novel recognizes have a closed texture.

There are however similarities between the concept of the self given here and that of the earlier novels. There is the same criticism of the arid intellectualism associated with Breadalby in *Women in Love*. Clifford's set is caught in the same critical light as the guests at Breadalby. In their discussions on love and sex they are revealed rather obviously as the opponents of Lawrence's own idea of the importance of the body in human relationships. For them mind is all important and sexual contacts are simply 'an interchange of sensations instead of ideas'.[1] Clifford's own conversation, though brilliant, is dead – 'not the leafy words of an effective life, young with energy that belongs to the tree'. He and his friends are the products of decadence, 'not manifestations of energy'.[2] Sex, for him, is nothing but an occasional excitement and not nearly so vital as those habits which form between people who live together in the same house for a long time without the need for physical intimacy.[3] Tommy Dukes contrasts the empty conversation of these intellectuals with 'real knowledge [which] comes out of the whole corpus of consciousness'.[4] Though it is a kind of knowledge from which he, as a member of this decadent society, is debarred and he confesses that talking to a woman puts him poles apart from her so far as any physical intimacy is concerned and consequently he is not really interested in sex.[5] Lawrence will counter this by emphasizing the importance of the body and the emotions in the rediscovery of the natural self and its contacts 'with the substantial and vital world'.[6]

Another familiar enemy of the natural self is industrialization. For industrial life and the mechanical principle it incorporates are identified as another major element in the destruction and redefinition of the self, causing that 'gap in the continuity of consciousness' which makes life so intolerable to Connie and Mellors.[7] Clifford in his motorchair is a gruesome symbol of this new nature; cut off by choice and misfortune from a wholly integrated life, he turns for refuge first to his intellectual friends and his writing and then to the management of the mines. Here he achieves a sense of power and a satisfaction from which his physical impotence has always debarred him. But the mines are inhuman and Mellors reflects on 'those evil electric lights and diabolical rattlings of engines' and upon the natures which such forms of life create.[8] 'It was a world of iron and coal, the cruelty of iron and the smoke of coal, and the endless, endless, greed that drove it all.'[9] As in *Women in Love*, we are asked to contemplate the re-formation of human nature and its adaptation to the needs of new and more efficient modes of production. It is creating a new race of men, Connie reflects in her journey across the industrial wasteland, in whom the intuitive faculty is dead and the possibilities of fellowship and conviviality erased.[10] The self has become a by-product of industrial life; its new structures a prison in which spontaneous life is impossible, and the novel is a planned escape through the phallic consciousness.

It is at this point that Lawrence's view of the fully achieved individual begins to change, as some of the tensions and paradoxes of the earlier concept are discarded. Mellors, in any sense which the earlier novels or the criticism would have recognized, is a renegade. He is a man who had access to the social world of education and culture and who turns his back on it to live in another, where his connections with nature are closer while his connections with the civilized world are reduced to a minimum. His relationship with Connie represents a rejection of a whole area of conscious being as that was defined by the earlier novels and it implies a diminished concept of the self. He gets away with this to some extent by carrying with him the cultured poise of the world he repudiates. He is never just a gamekeeper and the novel is at pains to point this out. We are told he had a scholarship for Sheffield Grammar School and that he 'learned French and things';[11] he had a little French and German and read poetry;[12] he and his first girl were 'the most literary-cultured couple in ten counties';[13] and eventually when he takes a job as a farm labourer he is able to help his landlady's daughter who is training for a school teacher. [14] Finally when Connie sees him for the first time in London he does not quite have the cut to pattern look but he has a natural distinction in his formal suit and she sees at once that 'he could go anywhere'. [15] These remarks testify to an uneasiness in Lawrence which refuses to turn renegade on the civilized world. But it occurs in a work which came into being, we are told, with the sentence, 'Civilized society is insane.' [16] And Mellors is presented in the book as the enemy of any cultured or civilized society which the book acknowledges. But *Studies* and the major novels have made it clear that there can be no going back and that we cannot abandon the struggle into conscious being in the way Mellors does. We have only to contrast him with Birkin to see where the failure lies. For Birkin too is a critic of the cultured world in which he lives but, though he is often tempted to, he does not turn his back on that world completely. There is always in him that final tolerance which Ursula noted. He realizes that a total rejection of the world of culture is in effect a rejection of his humanity. He cannot become like the young man in the chapter, 'A Chair'. Not the rejection of all culture but a process of discrimination within it becomes his task. Birkin remains a part of the civilized world because it is within a civilized culture that those conditions obtain in which the artist, the philosopher and the saint, to use Nietzsche's trinity, can flourish and transmit the world they create for each other and its life. Neither Birkin nor Lawrence is prepared to turn his back on that world. Like Goethe they recognize the debt they owe:

> People are always talking about originality; but what do they mean? . . . What can we call our own except energy, strength, and will? If I could give an account of all that I owe to great predecessors and contemporaries, there would be but a small balance in my favour. [17]

Lawrence's debt to predecessors and contemporaries is evident and frequently testified to; we have seen already the community to which he belongs. For Mellors there is no community; civilized society is completely insane and one must escape it into the private world of the phallic consciousness. He does not 'believe in the world, nor in advancement, nor in the future of our civilization'. [18] Nevertheless, in a finicky kind of way, he must claim his inheritance and draw upon the culture he repudiates. It is in essence a mistake about the nature of the self and its connection with those common modes of thought and experience which are constitutive of it. The social and the private selves are not separate and from time to time the old awareness of this breaks through.

> Living is moving and moving on. My life won't go down the proper gutters, it just won't. So I'm a bit of a waste ticket by myself. And I've no business to take a woman into my life, unless my life does something and gets somewhere, inwardly at least, to keep us both fresh. A man *must* offer a woman some meaning in his life, if it's going to be an isolated life, and if she's a genuine woman. I can't be just your male concubine.[19]

But having abandoned the passionate struggle into conscious being and having severed his ties with the great world of responsible work, can he really be anything else? Connie says that his significance lies in that he has the courage of his own tenderness[20] and this is good, but the complex problems of contemporary industrial life can no more be solved by this formula than they can by the older Christian one which tells us, 'Love thy neighbour'.

And at the end of the novel the old insistence on the need for community reasserts itself as Mellors, in a letter to Connie, tries to formulate his concept of Utopia. People will have to be re-educated to live instead of to earn and spend. Then the men will wear scarlet trousers and amuse the women and be amused by them and they will 'dance and hop and skip, and sing and swagger and be handsome' and they will worship the great god Pan.[21] It is a delightful picture derived in part from Lawrence's studies of the tomb paintings at Cerveteri and Tarquinia. But we cannot take it seriously as a substitute for that living, believing community which is required and nothing in the novel suggests that there is any possibility of such a community in which the true freedom of the self could be realized. As a result Connie and Mellors are retreating into an impasse where the conditions of that freedom can never be found. Hence the fear with which Mellors contemplates the future and of having a child. And Connie too falters: 'She wanted to hide her head in the sand: or, at least, in the bosom of a living man. The world was so complicated and weird and gruesome.'[22] And in the end both do hide their heads in the sand.

Allied to this is the place given to the phallic consciousness in the novel. Sex can be seen in either of two ways. First there is Clifford's view, which is a modern version of dualism. Since only the intellect is important sex is merely a side-show, simply a matter of excitement and sensations and whether you get your thrills from intellectual conversation, as Clifford does, or from sex, as some of his friends do, is really of no importance. Hence he is prepared to encourage Connie to go and have an affair in Venice to produce an heir for Wragby. He can do this because for him the sex-thing is merely sensational and has nothing to do with what he calls the integrated life – 'the long living together of two people, who are in the habit of being in the same house with one another.'[23] According to Clifford no mere sexual affair could have any effect on Connie's relationship with him which is based on more solid ground.

Lawrence, on the other hand, a critic of dualism, maintains that sex is an essential element in the integrated life. This is expressed nowhere more lucidly than in his essay *A Propos of Lady Chatterley's Lover*, where he attacks the views of G. B. Shaw, seeing in them the same playboy mentality he had already diagnosed in Clifford. When Shaw suggests that we can learn more about sex from the Chief Prostitute of Europe than from the Chief Priest of Europe, Lawrence rightly retorts that this is only if we are speaking of counterfeit sex, i.e. the kind of sex which is merely about getting thrills. But once you replace sex in its natural and social context the reverse is the case.

> The Chief Priest of Europe knows more about sex than Mr Shaw does, anyhow, because he knows more about the essential nature of the human being. Traditionally he has a thousand years' experience.[24]

When the sexual dimension of man is understood as a part of his essential nature then there are other issues to be considered than sensations, issues which can only be understood within the kind of tradition which Lawrence indicates.

Its point of reference must not be those shallow desires with which Shaw is concerned but desires which are more profound and permanent and 'the Church is established upon the recognition of some, at least, of the greatest and deepest desires in man'.[25] One of the deepest of such desires is the desire for fidelity:

> All the literature of the world shows the prostitute's ultimate impotence in sex, her inability to keep a man, her rage against the profound instinct of fidelity in man, which is, as shown by world history, just a little deeper and more powerful than his instinct of faithless sexual promiscuity.[26]

This is that 'law of creation' to which Birkin referred when he demanded from Ursula a bond and maintained that their union must be irrevocable.[27] It is what is lacking in Shaw and the Chief Prostitute. In this way the essential nature of the self is intimately bound up with its position in society and as a result marriage is essential.

> It we are to take the Nonconformist, protestant idea of ourselves: that we are all isolated individual souls, and our supreme business is to save our own souls; then marriage surely is a hindrance . . . [but] supposing . . . I see the soul as something which must be developed and fulfilled throughout a life-time, sustained and nourished, developed and further fulfilled, to the very end; what then?[28]

Such development and fulfilment and the freedom it implies demand for Lawrence the security of an irrevocable union and involvement in a living, believing community. The nucleus of such a community is marriage, not as a property contract, but as a living bond between two people which also situates them in the wider community.

The larger community remains undefined. It is still essential that it should not be a community which would seek to redefine man in terms of the mechanical principles of industry nor in terms of the economics of greed. It must embody a reverence for human nature, in other words a community established like the Church upon the greatest and deepest desires of man and on their connection with the larger world of nature or the cosmos. The Church achieves this through its insistence on marriage and in its liturgy:

> . . . with the sunrise pause for worship, and the sunset, and noon, the three great daily moments of the sun: then the new holy-day, one in the ancient seven-cycle: then Easter and the dying and rising of God, Pentecost, Midsummer Fire, the November dead and the spirits of the grave, then Christmas, then Three Kings. For centuries the mass of people lived in this rhythm under the Church . . . . Now you have a poor, blind disconnected people with nothing but politics and bank-holidays to satisfy the eternal human need of living in ritual adjustment to the cosmos in its revolutions, in eternal submission to the greater laws.[29]

And it would seem that only a community like the Church could satisfy the conditions which his concept of the self demands. For it has in its traditions that which refuses to hand over the redefinition of man to any industrial or political project because it is grounded upon the recognition of creative sources in man and in the world which are mysterious and finally indefinable. From such a source should flow a concept of the self which is open and unlimited. However the practice of the Church has often fallen short of this ideal and though Lawrence did believe that it might form the basis of a community which could regenerate the insane society depicted in *Lady Chatterley* ('I think . . . that the Roman Catholic Church as an institution, granted of course some new adjustments to life, might once more be invaluable for saving Europe: but not as a mere political power')[30] it is unlikely that all the adjustments he had in mind could ever be made.

Now while Clifford's view of sex is sensational, the view of Connie and Mellors is supposed to be of the other kind. For them sex is an essential element in the growth of the self. It is for Connie an answer to 'the anguish of her generation's forlornness'.[31] And when they come together sexually this is nothing separate from that 'spirit of respect for the struggling, battered thing which any human soul is'.[32] And Connie, we are supposed to feel, changes and develops in her very nature as her sexual initiation proceeds.

But what in fact do we observe? It is true she becomes a little less neurotic and more illuminated and confident in her opposition to Clifford and his world. Again, in her passage 'through all the stages and refinements of passion'[33] she becomes less ashamed of her own body and its feelings and to that extent more integrated. But beyond this there are no developments. As a result we are given page after page of erotic description with very little point, beyond the experience itself of the sensations involved, and so the picture of sex given begins to gravitate towards the very sensationalism Lawrence was criticizing.

There are two reasons for this. Firstly, the idea of the phallic consciousness here is without a social dimension and consequently helps to sustain the illusion of the private self, finding its fulfilment apart from the society in which it has been structured and formed. Therefore Connie and Mellors can only return to one another again and again, and we witness no developments beyond, because there is no beyond. And secondly, the idea of the phallic consciousness seems to have become a fixed idea with Lawrence now. As a result the self it depicts is closed and as big a dummy in its own way as was the self of Benjamin Franklin. He has allowed his own past conceptions to petrify and then impose upon his creative talents, just as Birkin feared the art of the past would impose upon us now if it were not open textured.

Once again the attitude to language in the book is crucial to all these issues. Consider first Connie's long reflection on language in chapter 6:

All the great words, it seemed to Connie, were cancelled for her generation: love, joy, happiness, home, mother, father, husband, all these great, dynamic words were half dead now, and dying from day to day. Home was a place you lived in, love was a thing you didn't fool yourself about, joy was a word you applied to a good Charleston, happiness was a term of hypocrisy you used to bluff other people, a father was an individual who enjoyed his own existence, a husband was a man you lived with and kept going in spirits. As for sex, the last of the great words, it was just a cocktail term for an excitement that bucked you up for a while, then left you more raggy than ever. Frayed! It was as if the very material you were made of was cheap stuff, and was fraying out to nothing.[34]

Language, Connie sees, is the very stuff, the structure of the self and when it becomes debased then it really is the material of which we are made which becomes cheap. And since language is a public activity, the health of the individual self is determined by the health of the whole society which speaks it. The forms of life determine the state of the language and the language then returns to over-determine the forms of life, setting the horizons of the possible. Connie, like many of her Lawrentian predecessors, is horrified at this tyranny of language. She feels this imposition again when Clifford addresses a few apple-blossoms she has given him as 'Thou still unravished bride of quietness'. Somehow she feels the reality has been by-passed in Clifford's verbalization. When things are turned into words, then the common experience of society comes between the perceiver and his object robbing it of its unique life.

She was angry with him turning everything into words. Violets were Juno's eyelids, and wind-flowers were unravished brides. How she hated words, always coming between her and life: they did the ravishing if anything did: ready-made words and phrases, sucking all the life-sap out of living things.[35]

But, as we have seen, it is not the word itself which is to blame but the ready-made word and the hackneyed phrase which has become the meeting place of the community. Our experience is irrevocably bound up with language. But in the hands of the novelist and the poet, when they are really being novelists and poets, its effects are invigorating and liberating. It reorganizes and illuminates experience, creates it in a way only possible with language users. It is wrong, therefore, to mourn our involvement in a common language, for with all its dangers it is the condition of everything human. What, therefore, is required is a better theory of language and an ever improved and flexible way of using it and this is the only real alternative to the stereotype against which Connie reacts.

But no such alternative is presented in *Lady Chatterley's Lover*. Mellors, quite consistent with his desire to turn his back on civilized society, tries also to abandon its language and reverts to the Derby dialect and what Lawrence calls 'the shocking words'. In the study of *Women in Love* we saw that language was the Trojan horse which carried society into the most remote retreat of the individual self. In this way Mellors hopes to escape Birkin's dilemma; the great words have been soiled and so he will not use them. But this cannot work. For in doing so he abandons the struggle for verbal consciousness which Lawrence identified with the passionate struggle into conscious being. In Mellors the use of dialect is degenerate and becomes merely irritating. Connie's sister Hilda finds it exasperating. 'It sounds a little affected,' she tells him when they first meet and then she reflects: 'He was no simple working man, not he: he was acting! acting!'[36] And this is surely true and it cannot achieve the liberation for the self which Mellors intends. For the dialect and the dialect words have been soiled by their own history and it is sheer romanticism to think that the forms of life to which they restrict us are any broader than the alternatives derived from the language of the cultured middle class. The solution is not to be found in discovering an alternative prison for the self in an alternative set of concepts but in making use of the fullest resources of language, as an intelligent artist like Lawrence can, and thereby breaking the hold of every set of hackneyed words and phrases.

Words come to us with the whole history of the forms of life in which they have been used and as we use them we are initiated into those forms of life. But once we have learned them we can then go on to extend and develop their uses, placing them in new contexts and throwing them into new relations. In this way we revitalize them. However we can never obliterate their history, as many German writers discovered after the war. Lawrence attempted to tear the shocking words away from what had become their home in dirty jokes and bar-room conversations. For he wanted them restored to what he thought was their natural home where they form an indispensable part of the tenderness of sexual experience.

Trying to explain the use of the shocking words in *Lady Chatterley's Lover*, Lawrence tells us that

> . . . real culture makes us give to a word only those mental and imaginative reactions which belong to the mind, and saves us from violent and indiscriminate physical reactions which may wreck social decency. In the past, man was too weak-minded, or crude-minded, to contemplate his own physical body and physical reactions that overpowered him. It is no longer so. Culture and civilization have taught us to separate the reactions. We now know the act does not necessarily follow on the thought. In fact, thought and action, word and deed, are two separate forms of consciousness, two separate lives which we lead.[37]

And he goes on to propose an achieved harmony between these two. Lawrence's central point here is good. Real culture through language transforms what without it would remain mere indiscriminate reactions. As Schiller put it, Nature created man, but culture makes him human. Again that integrity which he recommends is healthy and spacious. But the language in which he expresses this is misleading, suggesting that words can be *given* meanings and that thought and action, word and deed, are separate forms of consciousness. Words and *human* deeds are inextricably bound up in the forms of life where they are found. Wittgenstein has demonstrated this point tirelessly. For instance, in his remarks on the human phenomenon of hope:

> A dog believes his master is at the door. But can he also believe his master will come the day after to-morrow? – *And* what can he not do here? – How do I do it? – How am I supposed to answer this? Can only those hope who can talk? Only those who have mastered the use of language. That is to say, the phenomena of hope are modes of this complicated form of life.[38]

And this reflection can be extended throughout the whole of human experience and language. For example, I can only distinguish things like flirting, courting, seducing, wooing, fornication, adultery, in language and therefore I can only perform any one of these deeds when I understand something of the language games in which they belong. Deeds are not separate from our modes of conceiving them. And words, too, are deeds, as Mellors knows. For he knows that speaking words is part of 'the deed of life' through which he expresses his tenderness for Connie.

Once more it is the way we conceive and use language that is important. There is no substitute for the persistent, intelligent discrimination which carries on 'the battle against the bewitchment of our intelligence by means of language'. Dialect by itself, and the obscene words are merely gimmicks and they do nothing to advance the struggle into conscious being to which Lawrence was committed. In this sense *Lady Chatterley's Lover* is a dead-end. It is a dead-end because the author has allowed a now petrified concept of the phallic consciousness to impose upon him, has fixed the self in a static mould which fails to take seriously its own social dimensions and in some respects has renegued upon the theory of language implicit in the earlier novels.

7 Conclusion: Language and Liberation

Lawrence's novels, then,

> . . . are not little theatres where the reader sits aloft and watches – like a god with a twenty lira ticket – and sighs, commiserates, condones and smiles . . . that's what my books are not and never will be . . . whoever reads me will be in the thick of a scrimmage.[1]

His art is moral in that it contains throughout a certain conception of what it means to be human, a certain view of the self. This view, as we have seen, is subject to continual revisions but it is there nevertheless and its essential contours remain the same.

These appear somewhat abstractly in *Studies in Classic American Literature*, where he gives us, as he says, his *Weltanschauung* and they are subjected to criticism and development in the major fiction. In *Studies* on the one hand he insists that the self is essentially social and cannot develop outside a living, believing community and on the other, he explores all those ways in which society, through its values, its norms, its language drives the individual self into different modes of inauthenticity and erodes its freedom. But this freedom does not consist, as Sartre and some other Continental philosophers have suggested, in choosing and creating our own values from nothing, but in 'educating' ourselves to respond spontaneously to the deepest sources of our own natures, the creative principle, the dark forest. The great barrier to such an education is the emphasis in Western society on the dominance of abstract thought and the ensuing desire to act only from those dimensions of the self which can be imprisoned within a set of human concepts. In opposing this view Lawrence insists upon the importance of the body and of an integrated view of the self which spills over any closed conceptual picture of it.

These views, which Lawrence held more or less intact throughout his life, then invade the novels and are subjected to that kind of examination and criticism which he believed to be the unique prerogative of creative fiction. However we must not think of this process chronologically. Some of the novels were written before, some during, and some after the creation of *Studies* and the interaction between it and the fiction is much more complex than the simple picture here suggests. But since Lawrence is first and last a novelist, it is in the novels that the important developments occur.

Even in the early novels Lawrence possesses a tentative grasp of those problems which are to dominate the major fiction. In both *The White Peacock* and *Sons and Lovers* he exposes a hostility towards a fully integrated self, first in the romantic idealism of Lettie and then in the stronger puritan spirituality of Gertrude Morel. Both are possessed by certain limiting conceptions of the self derived from the society and culture in which they have grown up. In these books the positive dimensions of social and cultural life are rather dimly apprehended. Lettie has a certain ethereal charm and an aristocratic courage and Mrs Morel a strong moral seriousness – a quality which Lawrence himself never lost. And, of course, there is Paul's painting. But set beside the effects of other socially derived ideas in the novel these constructive social elements are slight in their influence. With *The Rainbow*, however, the conflict between the individual self and the good citizen becomes central and the book illuminates again and again the importance of the social infrastructure of the self; first with the women of the Marsh, later in the failure of Will Brangwen to acquire that level of articulation through which he can realize his early aspirations and finally in the long struggle of Ursula to find her place in the world of responsible work. The book is a battle to integrate the demands of the social and the individual self; though it ends and no integration has taken place. Nevertheless the demands of both are more clearly realized here than anywhere else in Lawrence's fiction. In *Women in Love* the social and the natural self are examined in what Lawrence has now come to see as their most important meeting places; in society itself – Shortlands and Breadalby – in art and culture and in human language. Each, so long as its horizons are closed, is seen as an unhealthy habitat for the self. This happens in a society where certain fixed modes of human excellence are operative. It happens in art when the contours of its products are seen as final and complete and throughout all it happens where language is deprived of its open texture. Nevertheless the social infrastructure of the self cannot be dispensed with, and therefore none of these places of human culture can be abandoned. But in each, the self must remain aware of the horizon – the darkness beyond the circle of light – and the language it speaks must retain an open texture. And then in *Lady Chatterley's Lover* there is a retreat from these principles. The social infrastructure of the self is ignored, language is torn from its social context, its contours closed and the novel itself is narrowly didactic and as a work of art lacks that openness which Birkin found so essential in art if it was not to become oppressive.

Many difficulties unearthed in this study converge upon the problem of language and it is necessary in conclusion to say something about the philosophy of language and in particular the concept of open texture as it bears on these problems.

In the early part of this century the theory of language in England was dominated by the paradigm of scientific rationalism. This view found one of its best expressions in Wittgenstein's *Tractatus*. As we saw earlier, it was a view of language in which scientific propositions alone were considered meaningful. This is sometimes called the picture theory of language. The idea came to Wittgenstein when observing the procedures in a French courtroom where a model was constructed to illustrate some point about an accident. Each element in the model (a pram, a car, a pedestrian, etc) referred to a similarly placed element in reality. This, Wittgenstein thought, was a good analogy of language. Sentences are like pictures and each element in the picture stands for an element in the real world. To decide whether a picture is true or false 'it is laid against reality like a measure'.[2] His slogan at this time was: 'What can be said can be said clearly, and what we cannot talk about we must pass over in silence.'[3] And the philosopher's job was to clean up language, removing from it all those words which failed to pass the test of referring to 'facts' in the world as the picture model prescribed. The meaning of words, their boundaries, were strictly limited by the facts to which they pointed. Such a view could never accommodate the notion of open texture towards which Lawrence was working. Indeed it served merely to confirm his worst forebodings about the restricting influence of philosophy. However Wittgenstein's merit over virtually all his contemporaries was, as we have seen, that at the risk of fracturing the internal consistency of his theory he retained the concept of 'the mystical' which insisted that there was an area outside language which was free from the kind of limits indicated by the picture theory. It was, however, a place over which one had to pass in silence.

In 1929 Wittgenstein returned to Cambridge and began the process of dismantling the language theory of the *Tractatus* and he produced, as we have seen, a completely new view of the structure of language, richer and infinitely more sensitive to the myriad ways in which human language is actually used. He begins now to speak, not of language, but of different language-games. The philosopher is no longer to prescribe in advance how language ought to be used, rather he must now look and see how it *is* used. 'Don't think,' he warns, 'but look!'[4] And when he himself does begin to look at the vast complexity of ordinary language he realizes that no single theory of language devised *a priori* by philosophers will do.

But how many kinds of sentence are there? Say assertion, question, and command? – There are *countless* kinds: countless different kinds of use of what we call 'symbols', 'words', 'sentences'. And this multiplicity is not something fixed, given once for all; but new types of language, new language-games, as we may say, come into existence, and others become obsolete and get forgotten . . . .
Here the term 'language-*game*' is meant to bring into prominence the fact that the *speaking* of a language is part of an activity or a form of life.
Review the multiplicity of language-games in the following examples and in others:
Giving orders and obeying them –
Describing the appearance of an object, or giving measurements –
Constructing an object from a description (a drawing) –
Reporting an event –
Speculating about an event –
Forming and testing hypothesis –
Presenting the results of an experiment in tables and diagrams –
Making up a story; and reading it –
Playing–acting –
Singing catches –
Guessing riddles –
Making a joke; telling it –
Solving a problem in practical arithmetic –
Translating from one language into another –
Asking, thanking, cursing, greeting, praying.
It is interesting to compare the multiplicity of the tools in language and of the ways they are used, the multiplicity of kinds of words and sentences, with what logicians have said about the structure of language. (Including the author of the *Tractatus Logico-Philosophicus*.)[5]

Like Lawrence, Wittgenstein is now saying that it is philosophers who force language into the strait-jackets which distort it. They imprison us within sets of concepts and the cure for this philosophical disease is a return to ordinary language in all its diversity. This is why he now says: 'There is not *a* philosophical method, though there are indeed, different methods, like therapies.'[6] And this is also why his later philosophy has been thought of more as an art than a science. Furthermore it is surely true, as Lawrence claims, that if the richness of language is resurrected in a return to ordinary language forms, the novel must hold a unique place in such a project. And this is what our investigations have revealed.

Again, with the realization of the diversity of language forms, Wittgenstein also comes to perceive the social dimension of language, that words cannot be understood outside 'the stream of life'. Language is not just a picture which stands over against reality and represents it; it is a part of an activity or a form of life itself. Our language-games are a whole series of widely different tools through which social life – that is, human life – comes into being and continues to exist. 'And to imagine a language-game means to imagine a form of life.'[7] Beings who used language forms widely different from our own would not just describe reality differently; the very reality of their lives and their experiences would be different also.

Under the influence of this kind of thinking Friedrich Waismann introduced the notion of open texture into English philosophy. Furthermore it was not introduced to account for the use of language in areas like ethics, religion or literature but rather for those empirical concepts which are at the very heart of science itself. Waismann was speaking about the logical positivist concept of verifiability, i.e. that the meaning of a statement is its method of verification. Most sentences we understand quite well without having to bother very much about their method of verification. For instance, we never have to advert to thinking about methods of verification with sentences like, 'My dog is sick' or 'My dog barks'. But if someone says, 'My dog can think' this novel combination of words causes us to wonder about its method of verification because it raises questions about the meaning of the word 'think'. We can imagine a discussion about whether some dog can think or not ending with the remark, 'Ah! that's what you mean by "think".'

The difficulty arises here, Waismann says, because of the open texture of most of our empirical concepts. The sentence 'There is a cat next door' looks unproblematic and all the terms in it seem to have a definite meaning. To verify it I simply have to go and look. But is this enough? Must I also touch the cat? Induce it to purr? What would I say later if the creature grew to a gigantic size? What if it showed examples of queer behaviour not normally associated with cats? Should I still say with confidence it was a cat?[8] What has happened here is, of course, that the word 'cat' is not bounded in all directions; it has an open texture. This is true even of scientific concepts like 'gold'. For when such concepts are introduced into our language we only limit them in certain directions for present purposes and we tend to overlook the fact that there are countless other directions in which they have not been defined. Most of our empirical concepts have this character: they are non-exhaustive because we cannot foresee in advance all the possible circumstances in which we shall wish to use them.[9]

All this derives from the essential incompleteness of empirical descriptions. If, for example, I am trying to describe my hand, I can give its size, shape, colour etc, or I can go on and give its chemical compounds, cells etc, but I never reach an end of the description. For however far I go, it is always logically possible to extend the description by adding some detail or other. 'Every description stretches, as it were, into a horizon of open possibilities: however far I go, I shall always carry this horizon with me.'[10] To sharpen our focus on this characteristic of empirical description we have only to contrast it with descriptions in mathematics. In geometry if I describe a triangle by giving its three sides, that description is complete and nothing can be added to it. But empirical concepts are open-textured because something unforeseen can always occur which forces us to use them in new and unusual contexts. Think, for instance, of the change which takes place in our understanding of phenomena when a new agent of Nature like electricity is discovered.[11]

Some of the muddles we get into here arise from our tendency to see words and the facts they describe as separate and distinct. This, as we have seen, is a misunderstanding especially when we are thinking of human life and human institutions. Waismann comments on the experience of hearing a clock strike in the night:

I have observed that when the clock strikes in the night and I, already half asleep, am too tired to count the strokes, I am seized by an impression that the sequence will never end – as though it would go on, stroke after stroke, in an unending measureless procession. The whole thing vanishes as soon as I *count*. Counting frees me, as it were, from the dark formlessness impending over me. (Is this not a parable of the rational?) It seems to me that one could say here that counting *alters* the quality of the experience. Now is it the same fact which I perceive when counting and when not counting?[12]

Again, think of a man from a tribe whose members count 'one, two, three, a few, many' and who on seeing a flock of birds says, 'A few birds' whereas I say 'Five birds'; or an ornithologist who says 'Three sparrows and two dunnocks'. Is the experience the same in each case? are the facts? and what are the facts here? The real world is not a simple given which we then try to picture in our language. For language itself participates in the constitution of the facts. Though this is not to say it creates them. 'Reality is undivided . . . language is the knife with which we cut out facts.'[13] But this cutting process is always in relation to some present purpose or purposes and so the word remains undefined in certain directions and this is what gives it an open texture. Think of the proceedings in a law court where the judge is sometimes asked not to recall what a word means (e.g. a concept like 'reasonable care') but to *decide*, at least in one direction, what it now means and shall mean hereafter.

Empirical concepts in contrast to mathematical concepts, then, have this open texture. Now if this is true of empirical concepts and empirical description it is true *a fortiori* of moral concepts and of our attempts to describe human nature. For here it is doubly true that we can never foresee all the circumstances, whether these circumstances are external or internal to the self, in which we shall wish to apply our words. Indeed the crisis of modern civilization has arisen in part from a change in these very circumstances which has caused some to wonder whether the opening up of the old concepts has not altered their 'essential meaning' so completely that we can no longer use them. Lawrence's novels are a sensitive reflection on this very process. And when Nietzsche talks about a new morality beyond good and evil and involving a revaluation of all values he has something like this in mind also. Though it is true that Nietzsche's revaluation and the new virtues which belong to his *Übermensch* have more in common with forms of traditional morality than he often admits.

Moral concepts are often closed by the refusal of people to recognize their open texture and this means a refusal to see the emergence of a new context which exposes directions in which they have not been defined. Think, for instance, of the concept 'justice' and the changes which occur in our understanding of it after the transition from a monarchic to a democratic society, or after the abolition of slavery. Often it is the closed texture of the concept which inhibits the expansion of the horizon. In a society where 'justice' is defined in terms of the proper relations between a subject and his king it becomes 'unjust' to try to create a society where this relationship no longer obtains. Thinking of slavery, one has only to look at *Huckleberry Finn* to see the overpowering influences of a closed system of language in making it almost impossible for Huck and Jim to establish a new relationship and an enlarged concept of justice. The conclusion of Huck's long dialogue in which he tries to explain to Jim about kings and queens and why Frenchmen speak French springs to mind: 'I see it warn't no use wasting words – you can't learn a nigger to argue. So I quit.'[14] But the novel *Huckleberry Finn* reinforces Lawrence's point; it re-opens concepts hitherto closed.

Each of these situations – and there are countless others – creates a new context for which the original word 'justice' was not defined. But since it was only defined in certain directions its texture should remain open and its application to these new contexts is always a matter of urgent concern in the growth of culture and civilization. But as Lawrence knows there are always those who in the exercise of power or because they feel more secure when they are fenced in by concepts whose total meaning is defined, refuse to acknowledge any new horizon. For them the open road is closed. But the meaning of a word can only be closed if the context within which it operates is closed as in mathematics. A good parable of this can be found in the story of the reverent astronomer who refused to look through Galileo's telescope to see a new planet because he knew it could not be there since it was not mentioned in the system of Aristotle. For both in scientific language and in moral language it is the closed systems which restrict our concepts and impede further developments.

Now, if we look again at Lawrence's debate with Benjamin Franklin we will see that what he is protesting against in Franklin is the latter's attempts to create a completely closed system of moral concepts and therefore a completely closed nature for the self modelled upon them. It is only in mathematics that concepts have this completely closed texture. The attempt to introduce such a texture into morals, philosophy and religion has been the bane of Western philosophy since Descartes announced his aspiration to bring to ethics and to philosophy in general the same kind of clarity and certainty which he found in mathematics.[15]

Twenty years after Descartes' death Spinoza's *Ethica, ordine geometrico demonstrata* was published in which he set out his ethics with definitions, axioms and propositions exactly in the manner of Euclid. This rationalist dream has occurred again and again in philosophy but it is misplaced because it misunderstands the essential difference between mathematical language and other language forms.

When Lawrence takes Franklin's list of virtues, like temperance, order, frugality, chastity, etc, and produces his alternative list he is trying, in effect, to prise open again concepts which Franklin has closed. Thus, for example, when Franklin defines moderation: 'Avoid extremes, forbear resenting injuries as much as you think they deserve,' Lawrence retorts: ·MODERATION Beware of absolutes. There are many gods.'[16] This is not a statement on Lawrence's part of polytheism. His intention rather, is to ensure that no single human concept of God, like Franklin's, shall dominate and determine the structure of the self. In his insistence on the gods and the dark forest, which runs throughout his own list of the virtues, Lawrence is making explicit in morality that horizon which Waismann says we must always carry about even in the domain of the positive sciences.

This study began by indicating some of the paradoxes in Lawrence's attitude to religion and many of these paradoxes can now be elucidated by the application of the view of language outlined in this chapter. His thoughts about religion changed throughout his life from an early theism to a repudiation of Christianity in 1915 when he wrote to Russell, very much under the influence of the pre-Socratic philosophers and in particular Heraclitus,

> I have been wrong, much too Christian in my philosophy. These early Greeks have clarified my soul. I must drop all about God . . . I am rid of all my Christian religiosity. It was only muddiness.[17]

And then, as we have seen, towards the end of his life he comes again to take a more sympathetic view of the Church and its liturgy as a community with a language which escaped in certain fundamental ways the limitations of other contemporary forms of human association. These changes are not so much the result of changes in Lawrence's attitude to the self and society as of a change in his focus on different aspects or different traditions within the Church. These changing attitudes also appeared in the novels. Earlier, as we saw, Christianity was seen as a puritan strait-jacket which confined the self in its purely intellectual or spiritual mode. It formed indeed the very closed horizon of which I have been speaking; and it imprisoned the self within the same rigid concepts. Then in *The Rainbow* Lawrence began to investigate a very different kind of religious language whose function was the reverse of that depicted in the earlier books. This was the language of transcendence, whose very nature is to insist upon the inadequacy of every form of language to completely encapsulate the reality of man and of the deity. Like every great religious tradition it both affirmed the authoritativeness and the relativity of its own representations. It was through her immersion in this kind of language that Ursula was saved from any narrowly circumscribed view of her self and her position in society which her father and mother tried to impose upon her.

The liberating view of open-texture language has a long established tradition within Christian theology which we need not probe in any detail. St Thomas Aquinas, for example, says of God, who is for him the primary referent of all moral terms like 'goodness', 'truth', 'justice', that 'what he is not is clearer to us than what he is' and so we must recognize 'how far above human speech and thought he is'.[18] And the corollary of this is that words like 'goodness', 'justice', and the structure of the self which they help to create can never be fully encapsulated within a definition but will always open upon an infinitely expanding horizon.

This is indeed Ursula's experience. She has a view of her own possibilities which spills over, or in the old language, transcends any particular cognitive framework in which she is asked to encounter it. And the language in which this vision is kept alive is the transcendent language of her religious experience. The dangers of her position, as we noted, lay in the tendency of that language to become so transcendent that it ceased to have any meaning at all. Now, perhaps a better way to express this would be to say that it lost its power to play any effective part in a significant form of life. It had become a private language because the community from which it had sprung and in which it flourished is given in the novel as something dead. It is a community which has surrendered its claims upon those daily forms of human intercourse where alone its words could engage reality and acquire a meaning in the stream of life.

Towards the end of his life, in *The Man Who Died*, a sort of parable based on the story of the risen Christ, Lawrence returns again to the religious theme. He depicts Christ after his death reflecting critically on his public ministry in which he had continually interfered with and imposed upon people, creating in them the lesser life of his own idealism and impeding the larger, freer life beyond. Now risen, he rejects this way and seeks in himself and others the realization of that self which transcends every ideal framework. In spite of the differences in the story between this and the New Testament there is a real affinity between the two. For the New Testament too depicts a man seeking to break out from the restricted view of the self embodied in the Law and urging those he meets towards the larger and freer self which both he and Lawrence call the Holy Spirit. For the Law interpreted by the orthodox Jewish leadership of his time is just the kind of closed language system which with its idealism becomes a prison of the self and impedes its transcendence.

The danger in the use of the language of transcendence arises when we assume that because we can find limits to any conceptual framework in which we try to grasp the self, we can therefore do without any framework at all. This is a mistake. For the self is only found, indeed is only constituted, in language, even in a language it transcends. As we have seen there is no archimedean point outside society or outside language to which we can escape. The relative ones we have are the only ones there are and they form the conditions in which political and social life become possible. But the view advanced here entails that while we affirm the necessity of some conceptual framework as a part of the struggle into conscious being, we must at the same time proclaim the relativity of that structure. This, as I have hinted, is the position of Jesus, who until his death remains an incorrigible iconoclast *within* the orthodox Jewish faith. Cut adrift from the social, religious and linguistic traditions of Judaism his work would disintegrate. Both Ursula Brangwen in *The Rainbow* and Birkin in *Women in Love* find their best selves in this polarity of affirmation and denial. But the temptation of Lawrence's work is always to resolve the paradox by denying the public world of culture, work and language and so to destroy that tension which is essential to the complex reality of the self.

It is in this context that Lawrence is quite right when he claims that 'art is utterly dependent on philosophy: or . . . on a metaphysic'.[19] And when he goes on to say that 'it is a metaphysic that governs men at the time, and is by all men more or less comprehended or lived',[20] he is drawing attention to the fact that the world and the self only come to be in some conceptual framework. The better that framework the better the possibilities for life and art in that time. But it is never complete and this is where the novel comes in. For it is never just a vehicle for some metaphysic, however comprehensive; rather it always involves an examination of it from within, in which its relativity is affirmed, the open texture of its basic concepts displayed and the transcendence of the self revealed.

Notes

CHAPTER 1

1. A. J. Ayer, *Language, Truth and Logic* (London (1936) 1962) pp. 107–8.
2. D. H. Lawrence, *Phoenix* (London, 1936) p. 533.
3. D. H. Lawrence, *Phoenix II* (London, 1968) p. 413.
4. D. H. Lawrence, *Fantasia of the Unconscious and Psychoanalysis and the Unconscious* (1923) (Harmondsworth, 1971) p. 15.
5. *Phoenix*, p. 537.
6. L. Wittgenstein, *Tractatus Logico-philosophicus*, translated by D. F. Pears and B. F. McGuinness (London (1922), 1961) paragraph 6.12.

CHAPTER 2

1. D. H. Lawrence, *Collected Letters*, edited by Harry T. Moore (London, 1962) p. 603.
2. D. H. Lawrence, *Studies in Classic American Literature* (New York, 1923) (London, 1964) p. 4.
3. *Ibid.*, p. 6.
4. *Ibid.*, pp. 18–19.
5. *Ibid.*, p. 10.
6. B. Russell, *Portraits from Memory* (London, 1958) p. 111.
7. S. Kierkegaard, *Fear and Trembling and the Sickness unto Death* (Copenhagen, 1843 and 1849) translated by W. Lowrie (New York, 1954) p. 77.
8. *Tractatus*, p. 3.
9. Benjamin Franklin, *The Autobiography* (1818) (New Haven and London, 1964).
10. D. H. Lawrence, *Women in Love* (New York, 1920) (Harmondsworth, 1960) p. 45.
11. James Fenimore Cooper, *The Deerslayer* (1841) (New York, 1963) p. 41.
12. *Studies*, p. 61.
13. Edgar Allan Poe, *Tales, Poems and Essays*, (1845) (London and Glasgow, 1952) p. 151.
14. *Ibid.*, p. 156.
15. D. H. Lawrence, *A Propos of Lady Chatterley's Lover and Other Essays* (London, 1930), (Harmondsworth, 1961) pp. 102–3.
16. *Studies*, pp. 80–1.
17. Immanuel Kant, *Groundwork of the Metaphysic of Morals* (1783), translated by H. S. Paton (London, 1948) p. 3.

18. *Studies*, p. 99.
19. Teilhard de Chardin, *Le Milieu Divin*, translated by Bernard Wall (London, 1960) pp. 58–9.
20. *Phoenix*, p. 431.
21. T. S. Eliot, *After Strange Gods* (London, 1943) p. 61.
22. *Studies*, p. 129.
23. *Letters*, p. 720.
24. Herman Melville, *Moby Dick* (1851), (Harmondsworth, 1972) p. 162.
25. *Studies*, pp. 162–3.
26. F. Nietzsche, *Twilight of the Idols and the Anti-Christ*, (1889, 1895), translated by R. J. Hollingdale (Harmondsworth, 1968) p. 101.
27. F. Nietzsche, *Gesammelte Werke* (Munich, 1920–9), in Walter Kaufmann, *Nietzsche: Philosopher, Psychologist and Antichrist* (New York, 1968) p. 80.
28. F. Nietzsche, *The Gay Science* (1882), translated by Walter Kaufmann (New York, 1974) paragraph 381.
29. F. Nietzsche, *Thus Spoke Zarathustra* (1883–5), translated by R. J. Hollingdale (Harmondsworth, 1961) I, 21.
30. F. Nietzsche, *The Will to Power* (1901), translated by Walter Kaufmann (New York, 1968) paragraph 493.
31. *Twilight of the Idols*, p. 34.

CHAPTER 3

1. D. H. Lawrence, *The White Peacock* (London, 1911), (Harmondsworth, 1950) p. 143.
2. *Ibid.*, p. 331.
3. *Ibid.*, p. 357.
4. *Ibid.*, p. 323.
5. *Ibid.*, p. 39.
6. *Ibid.*, pp. 42–5.
7. *Ibid.*, p. 82.
8. *Ibid.*, pp. 174–5.
9. *The Will to Power*, paragraph 579.
10. F. Nietzsche, *The Wanderer and his Shadow*, paragraph 322 (1880) in Walter Kaufmann, *On the Genealogy of Morals and Ecce Homo* (New York, 1969).
11. *The White Peacock*, p. 154.
12. *Ibid.*, pp. 255–6.
13. F. R. Leavis, *D. H. Lawrence: Novelist* (London, 1955), (Harmondsworth, 1964) p. 19.
14. D. H. Lawrence, *Sons and Lovers* (London, 1913), (Harmondsworth, 1948) p. 18.
15. *Ibid.*, p. 18.
16. *Ibid.*, p. 23.
17. *Ibid.*, p. 82.
18. *Studies*, p. 81.
19. *Sons and Lovers*, p. 18.
20. *Ibid.*, p. 19.
21. *Studies*, p. 69.

22. *Sons and Lovers*, p. 201.
23. *Ibid.*, p. 212.
24. *Ibid.*, p. 417.
25. *Ibid.*, p. 349.
26. *Ibid.*, p. 351.
27. Arthur Schopenhauer, *Essays and Aphorisms* (1851) translated by R. J. Hollingdale (Harmondsworth, 1970) p. 47.
28. The question of a possible influence of Schopenhauer on Lawrence is not at issue here, although Lawrence read Schopenhauer with care and apparently with some approval some time before 1908.
29. *Sons and Lovers*, p. 350.
30. *Ibid.*, p. 510.
31. *Ibid.*, p. 472.

1. D. H. Lawrence, *The Rainbow* (London, 1915), (Harmondsworth, 1949) p. 9.
2. *Studies*, p. 130.
3. *The Rainbow*, pp. 19–20.
4. *Ibid.*, p. 25.
5. *Ibid.*, p. 57.
6. *Ibid.*, p. 56.
7. *Ibid.*, p. 94.
8. *Ibid.*, p. 95.
9. *Ibid.*, p. 91.
10. *Ibid.*, p. 40.
11. *Ibid.*, p. 81.
12. *Ibid.*, p. 103.
13. *Ibid.*, p. 105.
14. L. Wittgenstein, *Philosophical Investigations*, translated by G. E. M. Anscombe (Oxford, 1953) para. 109.
15. *The Rainbow*, p. 103.
16. *Ibid.*, p. 114.
17. *Ibid.*, p. 115.
18. *Ibid.*, p. 128.
19. *Ibid.*, p. 129.
20. *Ibid.*, p. 144.
21. *Ibid.*, p. 149.
22. *Ibid.*, p. 169.
23. *Ibid.*, p. 158.
24. *Ibid.*, p. 173.
25. *Ibid.*, p. 167.
26. *Ibid.*, p. 171.
27. S. Kierkegaard, *Concluding Unscientific Postscript* (Copenhagen 1846), translated by D. F. Swenson (Princeton, 1941) p. 182.
28. *The Rainbow*, p. 206.
29. *Ibid.*, p. 238.
30. *Ibid.*, p. 236.

31. *Ibid.*, p. 237.
32. *Ibid.*, p. 264.
33. D. H. Lawrence *Apocalypse* (Florence, 1931), (Harmondsworth, 1974) p. 94.
34. *The Rainbow*, p. 269.
35. *Existentialism from Dostoevsky to Sartre*, edited by Walter Kaufmann (New York, 1956) pp. 163–4.
36. *Ibid.*, p. 165.
37. *Phoenix*, p. 608.
38. *Phoenix II*, p. 599.
39. *The Rainbow*, p. 277.
40. *Ibid.*, p. 280.
41. *Ibid.*, p. 281.
42. *Ibid.*, p. 341.
43. *Ibid.*, p. 321.
44. *Ibid.*, p. 322.
45. *Ibid.*, p. 326.
46. *Ibid.*, p. 326.
47. *Ibid.*, p. 344.
48. *Ibid.*, p. 358.
49. *Ibid.*, p. 391.
50. *Ibid.*, p. 9.
51. *Ibid.*, p. 405.
52. *Ibid.*, p. 425.
53. *Ibid.*, p. 406.
54. *Ibid.*, p. 406.
55. *Ibid.*, p. 416.
56. *Ibid.*, p. 417.
57. *Phoenix*, p. 616.
58. D. H. Lawrence *St Mawr* (London, 1922), in *St Mawr and The Virgin and the Gipsy* (Harmondsworth, 1950) p. 160.
59. *The Rainbow*, p. 417.
60. F. Nietzsche, *The Twilight of the Idols*, p. 101.
61. *The Rainbow*, pp. 434–5.
62. *Ibid.*, p. 435.
63. *Ibid.*, p. 435.
64. *Ibid.*, pp. 437–8.
65. *St Mawr*, p. 159.
66. *The Rainbow*, p. 436.
67. *Ibid.*, p. 430.
68. *Ibid.*, p. 450.
69. *Ibid.*, p. 452.
70. *Ibid.*, p. 450.
71. *Ibid.*, p. 498.
72. *Ibid.*, p. 485.

CHAPTER 5

1. *The Rainbow*, p. 91.
2. Gerald Vann, *On Being Human* (London, 1933).
3. D. H. Lawrence, *Women in Love* (New York, 1920), (Harmondsworth, 1960) p. 36.
4. *Ibid.*, pp. 43–4.
5. *Ibid.*, p. 45.
6. G. E. Moore, *Principia Ethica* (1903), (1962) p. 188.
7. *Women in Love*, p. 92.
8. *Ibid.*, p. 48.
9. *Ibid.*, p. 156.
10. *Ibid.*, p. 328.
11. *Ibid.*, p. 329.
12. *Ibid.*, p. 337.
13. *Phoenix II*, p. 276.
14. *Phoenix*, p. 757.
15. *Women in Love*, p. 36.
16. *Ibid.*, p. 256.
17. *Ibid.*, p. 260.
18. Lionel Trilling, *Sincerity and Authenticity* (London, 1974) p. 126.
19. *Phoenix II*, p. 275.
20. *Women in Love*, p. 87.
21. *The Twilight of the Idols*, Section I.
22. *Ibid.*, p. 29.
23. *Ibid.*, p. 33.
24. *Ibid.*, p. 33.
25. *Phoenix II*, p. 276.
26. *Women in Love*, p. 139.
27. *The Twilight of the Idols*, p. 95.
28. B. Russell, *Portraits from Memory*, p. 109.
29. *The Twilight of the Idols*, p. 104.
30. *Ibid.*, p. 102.
31. *Women in Love*, p. 191.
32. *Ibid.*, p. 323.
33. *Ibid.*, p. 206.
34. *Ibid.*, p. 367.
35. *Ibid.*, p. 65.
36. *Ibid.*, p. 248.'
37. *The Sunday Times Review*, 5 September 1976.
38. *Women in Love*, pp. 539–40.
39. *Ibid.*, p. 36.
40. *Phoenix II*, pp. 365–415.
41. *Ibid.*, p. 190.
42. *Women in Love*, p. 398.
43. *Phoenix II*, p. 397.
44. *Women in Love*, p. 60.
45. *The Twilight of the Idols*, p. 45.
46. *Women in Love*, p. 355.

47. *Ibid.*, p. 142.
48. A. Schopenhauer, *Essays and Aphorisms*, p. 47.
49. *Women in Love*, p. 144.
50. *Phoenix*, p. 429.
51. *Women in Love*, p. 140.
52. *Ibid.*, p. 143.
53. A. Kenny, *Wittgenstein* (Harmondsworth, 1973) pp. 160–1.
54. *Women in Love*, p. 162.
55. *Phoenix*, p. 757.
56. *Women in Love*, p. 209.
57. *Ibid.*, pp. 162–3.
58. *Ibid.*, p. 283.
59. *Ibid.*, p. 164.
60. *Ibid.*, p. 169.
61. W. Wordsworth, *The Prelude* (1805), (London 1933) xi, 97–8.
62. *Women in Love*, p. 283.
63. *À Propos of Lady Chatterley's Lover*, p. 105.
64. *Women in Love*, p. 199.
65. *Phoenix*, pp. 755–60.
66. *Ibid.*, pp. 758–9.
67. *Ibid.*, p. 760.
68. J. S. Mill, *Autobiography* (1873), (Oxford, 1971) p. 89.
69. *Women in Love*, p. 401.
70. *Collected Letters*, p. 466.
71. *Women in Love*, p. 403.
72. *Ibid.*, p. 402.
73. J. P. Eckermann, *Conversations with Goethe* (1846), (London, 1930) p. 379.
74. *Phoenix II*, p. 288.
75. *Women in Love*, p. 477.
76. *Ibid.*, p. 477.
77. *Ibid.*, p. 480.
78. *Ibid.*, p. 481.
79. *Ibid.*, p. 483.
80. *Ibid.*, p. 484.
81. *Ibid.*, p. 485.
82. *The Twilight of the Idols*, p. 81.
83. *Women in Love*, p. 400.
84. J. P. Sartre, 'The Childhood Leader', in *Intimacy and other Stories* (Paris, 1939), translated by L. Alexander (St Albans, 1960) p. 200.
85. *Existentialism from Dostoevsky to Sartre*, pp. 133–4.
86. *Ibid.*, p. 134.
87. *Ibid.*, p. 134.
88. D. H. Lawrence, *Mornings in Mexico and Etruscan Places* (London, 1932), (Harmondsworth, 1960) p. 144.
89. *Ibid.*, p. 149.
90. *Studies*, p. 165.
91. *Women in Love*, p. 233.

CHAPTER 6

1. D. H. Lawrence, *Lady Chatterley's Lover* (London, 1932), (Harmondsworth, 1960) p. 34.
2. *Ibid.*, p. 52.
3. *Ibid.*, p. 46.
4. *Ibid.*, p. 39.
5. *Ibid.*, p. 58.
6. *Ibid.*, p. 21.
7. *Ibid.*, p. 165.
8. *Ibid.*, p. 123.
9. *Ibid.*, p. 149.
10. *Ibid.*, pp. 158–9.
11. *Ibid.*, p. 151.
12. *Ibid.*, p. 208.
13. *Ibid.*, p. 209.
14. *Ibid.*, p. 313.
15. *Ibid.*, p. 287.
16. Mark Schorer, 'Introduction to *Lady Chatterley's Lover*' in *À Propos of Lady Chatterley's Lover and other Essays* (Harmondsworth, 1961) p. 127; and *Lady Chatterley's Lover*, p. 100.
17. J. P. Eckermann, *Conversations with Goethe*, p. 115.
18. *Lady Chatterley's Lover*, p. 290.
19. *Ibid.*, p. 289.
20. *Ibid.*, p. 290.
21. *Ibid.*, p. 315.
22. *Ibid.*, p. 165.
23. *Ibid.*, p. 57.
24. *À Propos of Lady Chatterley's Lover*, p. 102.
25. *Ibid.*, p. 105.
26. *Ibid.*, p. 103.
27. *Women in Love*, p. 103.
28. *À Propos of Lady Chatterley's Lover*, p. 108.
29. *Ibid.*, pp. 116–17.
30. *Letters*, p. 698.
31. *Lady Chatterley's Lover*, pp. 119–20.
32. *Ibid.*, p. 104.
33. *Ibid.*, p. 258.
34. *Ibid.*, p. 64.
35. *Ibid.*, p. 96.
36. *Ibid.*, pp. 254–5.
37. *À Propos of Lady Chatterley's Lover*, p. 88.
38. *Philosophical Investigations*, II, 1, p. 174.

CHAPTER 7

1. *Collected Letters*, p. 829.
2. *Tractatus Logico-philosophicus*, 2.1512.

3. *Ibid.*, Preface, p. 3.
4. *Philosophical Investigations*, para. 66.
5. *Ibid.*, para. 23.
6. *Ibid.*, para. 133.
7. *Ibid.*, para. 19.
8. F. Waismann, 'Verifiability', in *Logic and Language, First Series*, ed. by A. G. N. Flew (Oxford 1963), p. 119.
9. *Ibid.*, p. 121.
10. *Ibid.*, p. 122.
11. *Ibid.*, p. 124.
12. *Ibid.*, pp. 139–40.
13. *Ibid.*, p. 141.
14. Mark Twain, *Huckleberry Finn* (1884), (London, 1961) p. 86.
15. Descartes, *Discourses on Method* (1637), translated by A. Wollaston (Harmondsworth, 1960) p. 41.
16. *Studies in Classic American Literature*, pp. 12, 18.
17. *Collected Letters*, p. 352.
18. Aquinas, *Summa Theologiae* (1268–74), translated by T. Gilby (London, 1963) 1a, 1, ix, ad.3.
19. *Fantasia of the Unconscious*, p. 15.
20. *Ibid.*, p. 15.

Bibliography

Aquinas, St Thomas, *Summa Theologiae* (1268–74) Vol 2, translated by Timothy McDermot. Blackfriars, London, 1964.

Ayer, A. J., *Language, Truth and Logic*, London: Gollancz (1936), 1962.

Camus, Albert, *The Rebel* (Paris, 1951), translated by Anthony Bower. Harmondsworth: Penguin, 1953.

Clark, Colin, *The River of Dissolution*. London: Routledge and Kegan Paul, 1969.

Descartes, René, *Discourse on Method* (1637), translated by Arthur Wollaston. Harmondsworth: Penguin, 1960.

Eckermann, J. P., *Conversations with Goethe* (1846), translated by John Oxenford. London: Dent (Everyman's Library), 1930.

Eliot, T. S., *After Strange Gods*. London: Faber and Faber, 1934.

Flew, Anthony, *Logic and Language (First Series)*. Oxford: Basil Blackwell, 1963.

Jaspers, Karl, *Man in the Modern Age* (Berlin and Leipzig 1932). London: Routledge and Kegan Paul, 1933.

Kant, Immanuel, *Groundwork of the Metaphysic of Morals* (1783), translated by H. J. Paton. London: Hutchinson, 1948.

Kaufmann, Walter, *Existentialism from Dostoevsky to Sartre*. (Meridian books) New York: World Publishing Co., 1956.

——, *Nietzsche: Philosopher, Psychologist, Antichrist*. (Vintage Books) New York: Random House, 1968.

Kenny, A., *Wittgenstein*. Harmondsworth: Penguin, 1973.

Kierkegaard, S., *Concluding Unscientific Postscript* (Copenhagen, 1846), translated by D. F. Swenson. Princeton: Princeton University Press, 1941.

——, *Fear and Trembling and The Sickness unto Death* (Copenhagen, 1843), 1849, translated by W. Lowrie. New York: Doubleday, 1954.

Lawrence, D. H., *Mornings in Mexico* and *Etruscan Places* (London, 1927, 1932), Harmondsworth: Penguin, 1960.

——, *Three Novellas: The Fox, The Ladybird, The Captain's Doll* (London, 1923), Harmondsworth: Penguin, 1960.

——, *The Rainbow* (London, 1915), Harmondsworth: Penguin, 1949.

——, *Lady Chatterley's Lover* (London, 1932). Harmondsworth: Penguin, 1960.

——, *Women in Love* (New York, 1920). Harmondsworth: Penguin, 1960.

——, *Fantasia of the Unconscious* and *Psychoanalysis and the Unconscious* (New York, 1922, 1921). Harmondsworth: Penguin, 1971.

——, *St Mawr* and *The Virgin and the Gipsy* (London, 1925; Florence, 1930). Harmondsworth: Penguin, 1950.

——, *Apocalypse* (Florence, 1931). Harmondsworth: Penguin, 1974.

——, *Collected Letters*, ed. H. T. Moore. London: Heinemann, 1962.

——, *Phoenix*. London: Heinemann, 1936.

——, *Phoenix* II. London: Heinemann, 1968.

——, *Studies in Classic American Literature* (New York, 1923). London: Heinemann, 1964.

——, *The Woman Who Rode Away and other stories* (London, 1928). Harmondsworth: Penguin, 1950.

——, *The White Peacock* (London, 1911). Harmondsworth: Penguin, 1950.

——, *Sons and Lovers* (London, 1913). Harmondsworth: Penguin, 1948.

——, *Love Among the Haystacks and other stories* (London, 1930). Harmondsworth: Penguin, 1960.

——, *A Propos of Lady Chatterley's Lover and other Essays* (London, 1930). Harmondsworth: Penguin, 1961.

Leavis, F. R., *The Common Pursuit* (London, 1932). Harmondsworth: Penguin, 1962.

——, *D. H. Lawrence Novelist* (London, 1955). Harmondsworth: Penguin, 1964.

Marx, Karl, *Selected Writings in Sociology and Social Philosophy*, ed. by T. B. Bottomore and M. Rubel. Harmondsworth: Penguin, 1963.

Mill, John Stuart, *Autobiography* (1873). Oxford: Oxford University Press, 1971.

Moore, G. E., *Principia Ethica*. Cambridge: Cambridge University Press, (1903), 1962.

Nietzsche, Friedrich, *The Gay Science* (1882), translated by W. Kaufmann. New York: Vintage Books, Random House, 1974.

——, *The Genealogy of Morals* (1887) and *Ecce Homo* (1908), translated by W. Kaufmann. New York: Vintage Books, Random House, 1969.

——, *The Will to Power* (1901), translated by W. Kaufmann. New York: Vintage Books, Random House, 1968.

——, *Twilight of the Idols* (1889) and *The Anti-Christ* (1895), translated by R. J. Hollingdale. Harmondsworth: Penguin, 1968.

———, *Thus Spoke Zarathustra* (1892), translated by R. J. Hollingdale. Harmondsworth: Penguin, 1961.

———, *The Birth of Tragedy* (1872) and *The Genealogy of Morals* (1887). (Anchor Books) New York: Doubleday, 1956.

———, *Beyond Good and Evil* (1889), translated by R. J. Hollingdale. Harmondsworth: Penguin, 1973.

Otto, Rudolph, *The Idea of the Holy* (Breslau, 1917). London: Oxford University Press, 1923.

Postman, Neil, and Weingartner, Charles, *Teaching as a Subversive Activity.* Harmondsworth: Penguin, 1969.

Russell, Bertrand, *Portraits from Memory.* London: Allen and Unwin, 1958.

Sartre, Jean-Paul, *Intimacy and other stories* (Paris, 1939), translated by Lloyd Alexander. (Panther) St Albans: Granada Publishing Ltd., 1960.

———, *Being and Nothingness* (Paris, 1943), translated by Hazel E. Barnes. London: Methuen and Co., 1958.

Schopenhauer, Arthur, *Essays and Aphorisms* (1851), translated by R. J. Hollingdale. Harmondsworth: Penguin, 1970.

Spinoza, Baruch, *Ethica ordine geometrico demonstrata* (1633), translated by A. Boyle. London: Everyman's Library, Dent, 1910.

Teilhard de Chardin, *Le Milieu Divin* (Paris, 1954), translated by Bernard Wall. London: Fontana, 1960.

Trilling, Lionel, *Sincerity and Authenticity.* London: Oxford University Press, 1974.

Twain, Mark, *Huckleberry Finn* (1884). (New Windmill Series). London: Heinemann, 1961.

Vann, Gerald, *On Being Human.* London: Sheed and Ward, 1933.

Wheelwright, Philip, *Heraclitus.* London: Oxford University Press, 1959.

Wittgenstein, Ludwig, *Philosophical Investigations,* translated by G. E. M. Anscombe. Oxford: Basil Blackwell, 1953.

———, *Tractatus Logico-philosophicus,* translated by D. F, Pears and B. F. McGuinness. London: Routledge and Kegan Paul, 1961.

Index

tradition, 92–4, 97
Trilling, Lionel, 78

utilitarianism, 11–12, 61, 73, 96

Vann, Gerald, 73
Verga, Giovanni, 94

Waismann, Friedrich, 116–20
Whitman, Walt, 24–5

will, 16–17, 41, 44–5, 75, 82
mechanical will, 77–8, 80, 95
Wittgenstein, Ludwig, 1, 4–5, 11, 52,
  61, 88
  Philosophical Investigations, 5, 110,
    115–16
  Tractatus Logico-philosophicus, 4,
    11, 114
Wordsworth, William, 91–2
work, 36–7, 64–5, 70, 99–100, 113,
  122